The Warrior's Mirror

THE PATH TO PEACE

Sirshree

'Sirshree's writing forces you to hold up a mirror against yourself and helps you fortify your character and rethink your values in life'

-Dr. Kiran Bedi, Magsaysay Award winner

The Warrior's Mirror
The Path To Peace
By **Sirshree** Tejparkhi

Copyright © Tejgyan Global Foundation
All Rights Reserved 2010.

Tejgyan Global Foundation is a charitable organization
with its headquarters in Pune, India.

ISBN : 978-93-87696-67-9

Published by WOW Publishings Pvt. Ltd., India
First edition published in October 2010
Second reprint in February 2025

Printed and bound by Trinity Academy For Corporate Training Ltd, Pune

This book is the translation of the Hindi book titled
Swayam Ka Samna by Sirshree Tejparkhi.

Copyright and publishing rights are vested exclusively with WOW Publishings Pvt. Ltd. This book is sold subject to the condition that it shall not by way of trade or otherwise, be lent, resold, hired out, or otherwise circulated without the publisher's prior written consent in any form of binding or cover other than that in which it is published and without a similar condition including this condition being imposed on the subsequent purchaser and without limiting the rights under copyright reserved above, no part of this publication may be reproduced, stored in or introduced into a retrieval system, or transmitted, in any form, or by any means, electronic, mechanical, photocopying, recording or otherwise, without the prior written permission of both the copyright owner and the above-mentioned publisher of this book. Any person who does any unauthorized act in relation to this publication may be liable to criminal prosecution and civil claims for damages.

Although the author and publisher have made every effort to ensure accuracy of content in this book, they hereby disclaim any liability to any party for any loss, damage, or disruption caused by errors or omissions, resulting from negligence, accident, or any other cause. Readers are advised to take full responsibility to exercise discretion in understanding and applying the content of this book.

The world is not as it appears to you;

rather, it is as you are.

This book is dedicated to this world

—a mirror that shows man his true face,

and helps him get a glimpse of his real self.

Contents

	Preface	07
1.	Hercules Faces Himself: Investigating Guilt	09
2.	The First Task of Hercules: Slaying the Lion—Investigating Family Disharmony	19
3.	The Second Task of Hercules: Clearing the Stables—Investigating Work-Related Problems	43
4.	The Third Task of Hercules: Slaying the Birds—Investigating Everything that is Unjust and Unfair	66
5.	The Fourth Task of Hercules: Obtaining the Apple—Investigating Illness	102
6.	The Fifth Task of Hercules: Herding the Cattle—Investigating Thoughts	130
7.	The Sixth Task of Hercules: Reining the Mares—Investigating False Beliefs	156

Preface

INTRODUCTION TO THE STORY OF HERCULES

Hercules is a mythological figure—a hero, a legend, a demi-god, tales of whom abound in both Greek and Roman mythology. He is renowned for his superhuman power and for saving the world by slaying many dangerous monsters. He is depicted as the epitome of strength and valour in various paintings and stories. The most popular of these stories is that of the Twelve Labours of Hercules. The story goes that in a fit of madness induced by his stepmother, Hercules killed his children and his wife Megara. After his madness was cured, he realized what he had done and fled to the city of Delphi where he prayed to the god, Apollo to absolve him of his sins. As a result of his prayers, the Oracle of Delphi appeared before him and directed him to serve his stepbrother, King Eurystheus, for ten years and perform every task he was commanded to. This would absolve him of his sins, he was promised. Eurystheus felt very insecure with Hercules around, since he feared he might take over the throne. And so he devised ten incredibly difficult tasks, hoping to get rid of Hercules through one of them. He later added two more, saying that Hercules had cheated in two of the tasks, and thus they came to be known as 'The Twelve Labours of Hercules'.

These twelve tasks comprised killing the Nemean Lion, destroying the nine-headed Lernaean Hydra, capturing the Golden Hind of

Artemis, capturing the Erymanthian Boar, cleaning the Augean stables within a day, slaying the Stymphalian Birds, capturing the Cretan Bull, reining in the Mares of Diomedes, stealing the girdle of the Amazon queen, herding the cattle of the monster Geryon, fetching the apples of Hesperides and, finally, capturing Cerberus, the three-headed hound. Hercules executed each of these tasks with strength, finesse and wit. Philosophical and moral lessons can be learnt if one looks deeper into his death-defying, superhuman exploits. On completing these twelve tasks, Hercules continued his journey of valour till, in the end, he was immortalized and accepted as a god.

This book uses the story of the Twelve Labours of Hercules to talk about inner conflicts instead of external conquests. For instance, encountering the lion of the ego is more important and more difficult than facing a real lion. This story teaches the technique of exploring and investigating yourself to resolve inner conflicts and to transform yourself completely. This inner investigation is based on a profound truth: the root of all complaints that we have about others is hidden within ourselves. The world is our mirror.

The story in this book is imaginary. However, the concepts are immortal. Instead of twelve tasks, in this story Hercules carries out six, but transforms twelve characters in the process. The technique of self-exploration explained to the twelve characters, and especially to the twelfth one, is extremely important.

One
Hercules Faces Himself: Investigating Guilt

Hercules' motorcycle was moving like the wind, piercing the dark silence. The bone-chilling cold made the atmosphere even more sinister. His earlier altercation with Radha, his wife, was playing havoc with his thoughts. His mind was disturbed, and he felt lonely and miserable.

His thoughts were whirling faster than his bike. He revved it, hoping to diffuse the pain his thoughts were causing him, but to no avail. All his efforts to empty his mind of crazy thoughts were futile. At times, his thoughts outpaced him; at times, they kept him company. His constant thinking produced nothing but a mist of confusion. He felt as if his eyes were losing their power to see. Astride his speeding bike, zigzagging through the city streets, he turned towards the highway. Suddenly, he felt his bike hit something. He couldn't understand what had happened. A heart-rending scream followed, and a cold shiver ran down his spine. He pressed hard on the brakes. The bike screeched to a halt.

Beads of sweat appeared on his forehead and he forgot the chill of the night. He turned back to look. A woman's body was lying on the road in a pool of blood. All the thoughts that had been troubling him suddenly disappeared into thin air. Various emotions—disbelief, compassion, fear, guilt—stabbed him from within like sharp knives.

Before Hercules could grasp the situation and decide what to do, a crowd had gathered. People started shouting, 'Catch that man! Don't let him get away!' A bolt of current ran through his body. Within seconds, his mind figured out the exact plan of action. He decided that his welfare lay in getting away from the scene instantly. He gave the bike full throttle. It skidded a bit but then stabilized and he vroomed away.

Hercules had been heading to his friend's house, but the accident made him turn back. He was definitely shaken by the situation the situation. His thoughts returned to the blood-drenched, injured woman, writhing in pain. His mind was full of questions: Wouldn't it have been better if I had stopped to help her? Should I go back and take her to the hospital? But will she still be alive? The possibility of her dying left him chilled. He started seeing the bars of a prison cell.

Hercules was still in this bewildered state when he reached his empty home. He let himself in and slumped on his armchair. His hands were shaking. He couldn't control his mind and started mumbling to himself, 'Didn't I have enough trouble on my hands already? Now this accident has made things worse.' All his problems appeared before his eyes, one after another, like scenes from a movie. He felt a lump in his throat. 'I didn't want to hurt anyone. Then why has all this happened to me? Oh god! How will I live with that woman's blood on my hands? Please get me out of this mess!' He needed to take immediate action and decided to leave the city. Feeling remorseful, he swore to himself, 'Until I atone for my sins, I will not return.' He left his home, relations, business, belongings—everything. He took his money, locked his house and left. He was headed for the unknown, in order to wash away the sin that he had unknowingly committed, and to cool the fire of repentance burning inside him.

He wanted to, somehow, get rid of his guilt.

Hercules owned a large showroom of electronic goods that he ran in partnership with his friend. He was a successful man who lived a comfortable life. His wife Radha was a well-mannered, educated woman. They had two lovely children. But there was something about him that had made Radha move out, taking their children with her.

Hercules was a well-built man, full of self-confidence and always prepared for any eventuality. He was successful in the material world, but his wealth and strength had turned him into a haughty man who would get furious at every little thing. In those moments, he could not tell good from bad. Gradually, the poison of anger manifested in his body as migraines. Every now and then, he would get a terrible headache. During acute attacks of migraine, he would lose his power to think and his rage would reach its zenith. As a result of his angry outbursts he started losing, one by one, his near and dear ones. First, he lost all his friends. Then Radha too got fed up of his behaviour and left.

Whenever Hercules sat down to think about this, he would realize his mistakes. But the very next moment, his ego would rear its ugly head and he would go back to square one. He wanted to apologize to Radha but his ego wouldn't let him. He was getting on his business partner's nerves as well, because he did not know how to behave with clients and also because he defaulted on his delivery commitments. The store was incurring continuous losses. His business partner tried talking some sense into him, but to no avail. Gradually, he too started distancing himself. Hercules' fury and egotism had estranged him from all his neighbours, acquaintances, friends and relatives. Now, he was finding their indifference towards him distressing.

While driving today, he had been shaken by thoughts of his recent altercation over the phone with Radha to such an extent that he had, possibly, become the cause of a woman's death. This was what he was pondering when he reached the train station and sat in the waiting room. 'Do I really harm people? If not, then why do people avoid me?'

He felt it was time for some serious introspection. He had to find answers. He started digging deep within and, after a while, he realized the uncomfortable truth—that he was at fault. Initially, he could not accept it. But he knew it was the truth. And when he accepted it, a tremendous feeling of guilt overwhelmed him. 'I have hurt my own people! I have troubled them a lot. How could I be so selfish, egoistic and cruel? And how could I be so careless? I can't even imagine how that woman's family must be feeling right now! Oh god! What have I done? Please help me. Please help me…' he was devastated.

He didn't know how the night passed amidst the sounds of incoming and outgoing trains and the sharp whistling of train engines. As he gradually opened his eyes to look around, he was surprised that he could not see anything—just bright white light. It was a kind of light that he had never seen before. It looked otherworldly, celestial. And then he felt as if a goddess was standing in front of him. He felt giddy. He couldn't believe his eyes. He rubbed them to make sure he was not dreaming. The Goddess was still there. He immediately prostrated before her and started sobbing like a child. After a while he pulled himself together and pleaded, 'Mother, I am ashamed of all that I have done. I want to wash away my sins. Please help me.' The Goddess smiled and said, 'Look. Do you see the temple on top of that hill? Take refuge with the priest there. Serve him well. Obey him. He will assign you tasks to bring about a change in twelve people's lives in twelve months. That shall be your redemption.' Saying so, the

Goddess disappeared. Hercules muttered to himself, 'Bring about a change in people's lives! Who, me? I myself am burdened with my own sorrows. How can I be instrumental in transforming someone else's life? I am the one who needs help. This is beyond me… But wait! The Goddess herself has directed me!' He said to himself, 'Get up Hercules. Do not delay. You have to reach that temple.'

Suddenly, he woke up from his slumber and realised he was still in the station's waiting room. He understood that this was no ordinary dream. The Goddess had shown him the path to redemption. Hercules had, in the past, been directed by an inner voice from time to time, but he had always ignored it. Every person's conscience is his true teacher, but in his ignorance he often disregards it. Hercules too, because of his ego, had neglected the voice of his conscience. And that had landed him in his present state. Hercules' eyes opened to a newfound wisdom. He told himself, 'I shall never repeat these mistakes in my life. Let me try obeying the Goddess. There is no harm in going to the temple to see what happens.' Even the thought of it made him feel lighter.

Guided by intuition, he described the temple to the stationmaster and asked him whether he knew about such a temple and its whereabouts. Hercules was astonished when the stationmaster said that he did, and that it was in his native village. Having got the address of his destination, Hercules boarded the appropriate train. On reaching the village, he disembarked and inquired about the temple. He was told that there, indeed, was a temple atop a hill in this village. He started walking according to the directions he was given and reached the temple located far away, upon a hillock. It looked exactly like it had in his dream. He was surprised and pleased at how easily he had reached this place.

But there were still many questions in his mind. He stepped inside the temple cautiously. A priest was distributing offerings to the devotees. Hercules too joined the queue. The priest smiled at him and placed some fruit in his palms. Hercules bowed and sat down in a corner. One by one, all the devotees left the temple. Then, Hercules approached the priest. The priest smiled and asked, "Who are you? What is your name?" Hercules paid his respects to the priest and said, 'I am Hercules.'

'Hercules! What kind of name is that? What does it mean?' asked the priest.

'My name is actually Hari Kolse. But everyone calls me Hercules because of my build. You may know of the ancient Greek hero Hercules, known for his strength and courage.' Ignoring his explanation, the priest said, 'Well, Hercules, tell me… Where have you come from? I've never seen you in this temple before.' Hercules felt uncomfortable, but saw no other option—he told the priest his entire life story. He told him how he had committed sins, some knowingly and some unknowingly. In the end, he told him about his vision of the Goddess. As he related his story, Hercules' eyes became moist and his voice choked with emotion. He caught hold of the priest's hands and said, 'I want to live here. I want to serve you. I want to start a new life in the shelter of the Goddess.'

The priest, with his dark complexion, paunch and long tuft of hair, was a well-known figure. He lived in a small two-room shelter right next to the temple, while his family resided in the nearby village. Everyone respected him. But there was a dark side to the priest that no one knew—he was a corrupt and cunning man who used the sanctity of the temple to trade in intoxicants like opium, cannabis and marijuana. Thus, he was something else outside, and the complete opposite within.

Hercules was happy to have found the priest, but the priest cursed Hercules under his breath, 'Oh no! What a pain in the neck! I'm living as a priest to hide my illegal activities from the world and so far, no one has ever doubted me. The devotees don't suspect a thing. But if this man lodges himself at my doorstep, he'll come to know sooner or later.'

The priest cringed at the thought and almost snapped at Hercules, 'This is just your imagination. The Goddess doesn't appear to all and sundry! Besides, I'm doing fine by myself. I don't need an assistant or servant. I am a priest. I make do with whatever the devotees offer me. I spend all my time praying to the Goddess. I do not ask for anything more. You don't need to serve me. You should go somewhere else and look for a new life. You won't achieve anything by staying with me.'

But Hercules had seen this very temple and its premises in his dream. The Goddess herself had directed him to serve the priest. Hercules pleaded desperately, 'You may try to push me away, but I will continue to lie at your feet. You may not need me, but I won't leave any stone unturned in my devotion towards you. You may or may not like it, but I'm certain that this is what I must do.'

Hearing this, the priest's mind started racing, 'Oh Goddess! An unwelcome guest forcing himself on me! Maybe this man is crazy. But what if he is an undercover policeman or spy? He looks like a wrestler who can pound me to pulp if I refuse him.' He started feeling scared.

'What are you thinking, master? Please trust me. I won't be a burden to you. I have confidence in myself and I know that you will be happy with my services,' said Hercules with humility and servility.

Now the priest felt that he simply could not refuse. He would have to stop his nefarious activities for a few days and find some solution to this problem. 'All right! I can allow you to stay here on one condition,' he announced.

Hercules felt hopeful. 'What condition, master?'

'Whatever task I give you, you will have to complete it to my utmost satisfaction. If you can do that I shall keep you, otherwise I shall ask you to leave.' Hercules smiled, nodded and said, 'I'm ready to fulfil all your conditions.'

The priest allowed Hercules to stay in a rundown room behind the temple. He gave the responsibility of repairing that room to Hercules. Hercules was happy. Besides the various tasks allotted to him by the priest, he also took over the many small everyday chores—keeping the temple spick-and-span, tending to the garden, helping the priest in his rituals, cooking his meals, shopping for him and so on. Despite this, the priest was extremely unhappy. He was constantly mulling over how to get rid of Hercules. 'What impossible task should I assign to make him leave?'

One day, the priest saw a man sitting in a corner of the temple. By his clothes and manner he seemed like a respectable person from the nearby village. For the past few days, he had been coming to the temple early in the morning and leaving late at night, silently observing the daily routine and the comings and goings of people. The priest was worried. 'What does this man gain by sitting here all day?' He was taken aback when the man once stayed on through the night. 'Things are getting out of hand. Not just one, but two guys have decided to stay here! How will I carry on with my business?'

The following morning he spoke to the man. 'What is your name?' he asked. 'And why do you sit here all day? Don't you have anything to do?'

The man looked at the priest woefully and replied, 'My name is Jitendra. My family is such that...' his voice trembled. He controlled himself and then continued, 'I had a fight with my wife and my children some days ago. Since then, I have been very depressed. I do not feel like doing anything. I haven't even been to my office. Since there is no question of staying at home, I just come and sit here. Yesterday, things were so bad that I had to sleep here. You are the head priest of this temple. Please tell me how to solve my problem. I request you to come with me and put some sense into my wife's head. She is a great devotee of the Goddess. She will surely listen to you.'

The priest fell into deep thought. 'I'm not what this man thinks I am. How can I solve his problem? But if I refuse to help him, he will lose faith in the Goddess and there's no telling what he'll say to the other villagers about me!' Suddenly, a thought struck him. 'Why don't I send Hercules? I'm certain that Hercules won't be able to solve his problem. After all, he too has come here after fighting with his people. Then I can tell him that he hasn't passed the test and throw him out. Thus, I will kill two birds with the same stone! This villager will leave and Hercules too will have to vacate this place. That will be wonderful!' He was delighted with his plan. He told Jitendra, 'I'm completely responsible for this temple. That is why I cannot leave it even for one moment. But don't worry. I will send my disciple with you. He will assess the situation and find a solution to your problem.' 'Whatever you say!' Jitendra felt relieved.

The priest called Hercules who came running. 'Today, I'm assigning a very important task to you.' His opening words pleased Hercules. So far, the priest had not given him any task that would let him demonstrate his capabilities. The priest apprised him of the situation and said, 'You have to go to Jitendra's house, take account of the environment in his home and solve his family problem. This is not an easy task. And I hope you remember my condition.' Hercules nodded and said, 'Your wish is my command, sir.' But he felt unhappy. He'd thought that the priest would give him a task that would utilize his physical strength, but this was something else. 'What a dilemma! I had the same issues in my own home. That is why my family left me. Forsaking my wife, children, business and home, I came here. How can I help this man? Oh Goddess! What kind of test is this? Am I being a fool in following the dream? But what else can I do? I'll just have to wait and see where this takes me.'

With a spiteful smile, the priest asked, 'What are you thinking?'

'Oh, nothing,' replied Hercules and left to get ready for his journey.

Two
The First Task of Hercules: Slaying the Lion
—Investigating Family Disharmony

'Papa's here! Papa's here!' Jitendra's son and daughter ran towards him and hugged him.

'Where have you been? We've been waiting for you all night. Do you know how worried and anxious you had us? You've been staying out all day long for so many days now, but this is the limit. I cannot tolerate this any longer,' Jitendra's wife Jagruti burst out. Then her eyes fell upon Hercules and she checked herself.

Jitendra made a quick round of introductions. 'Meet Hercules. He is the priest's disciple at the temple of the Goddess. I stayed back at the temple last night. The priest has asked Hercules to help us in restoring peace and harmony in our home.'

Jagruti felt relieved upon hearing this. It was as if the Goddess had answered her prayers and sent an angel to help them out. In her heart, Jagruti expressed her gratitude to the Goddess. She showed Hercules to his room.

Jagruti served breakfast to the family. Then the children got ready and left for school. After his breakfast, Jitendra went to bed to get some sleep. Hercules started contemplating upon their home's environment and the behaviour of all the members. Suddenly, the image of his own wife and children appeared before his eyes. He felt sad and missed them terribly.

In the evening, Jitendra's children returned from school. They removed their uniforms, socks and shoes, and threw them carelessly along with their school bags. Then they freshened up, changed, had some refreshments and went out to play. They returned after an hour and started doing their homework.

Jitendra looked at the mess created by the children and yelled, 'Why don't you two ever keep your things in the proper place? Look how your shoes, socks, uniforms and toys are strewn all around. Haven't you learnt how to keep your space neat and tidy? I'm tired of telling you over and over again, but you don't even care. What's wrong with you two?' He didn't try to help the children in picking their stuff. He just kept shouting at them. His scolding ruined the children's mood. They could not concentrate on their homework any more. The whole atmosphere became tense.

At dinner time, everyone ate quietly. Jitendra wanted Jagruti to sit and chat with him and Hercules after dinner, but that didn't happen. She ate quietly, washed her hands and went off to sleep. Jitendra didn't like her indifferent behaviour. With bitterness in his voice, he told Hercules, 'Am I not justified in expecting my wife to talk to our guest for a while? But Jagruti can't even do this much. On the one hand I feel ashamed and on the other, I feel angry and frustrated. I'm very conscious of my behaviour in these matters. I know how to look after my guests.'

Hercules thought, 'I too had similar complaints against my family members. That is why I lost everyone. Looking at Jitendra's family, I feel that maybe our families think differently than us. The point is that we ourselves may also be making the same mistakes that we keep blaming them for!'

He wondered at this train of thought. Where was it coming from? How could he think these thoughts? It was another matter that he couldn't find the right words to make Jitendra see this point. In fact, he did not have the slightest clue about how he was going to solve this domestic problem. This was a difficult situation. However, he could not afford to fail in his very first task and so he fervently called out to the Goddess, 'Oh mother! I have followed your directions and started serving the priest. He has entrusted me with the task of restoring peace and harmony in Jitendra's home. But I cannot understand how to deal with the situation. Please throw some light on this problem.'

Suddenly Hercules heard a soft voice coming from within him. Hercules recognized it as the voice of the Goddess. It said, 'My blessings are always with you. Whenever you shall seek an answer, it will come from within you and you will be able to explain it in the most appropriate words. Whatever guidance you need will be provided to you.' Hercules felt happy and thanked the Goddess wholeheartedly for this blessing.

Jitendra was still carrying on, 'This kind of scene is repeated almost every day in our house. I have no peace of mind. Now only you can help us.'

Hercules replied, 'We are both tired right now. We'll get up early in the morning and go for a walk. That is when we'll discuss this matter.'

Jitendra said, 'But I have to go to my office tomorrow. I have already been absent for four days. Tomorrow I will have to leave early, otherwise my boss will get angry with me.'

Hercules offered a solution. 'That's all right,' he said. 'We can go for a stroll in the evening every day, after dinner. We'll discuss this matter then.'

The next morning Jagruti was preparing lunch boxes for Jitendra and the children. They took their bath, got ready for office and school, had their breakfast and left home. Before leaving, Jitendra told Hercules, 'There's a library nearby. It has a good collection of books. If you wish, you can borrow a book from there.'

Hercules could not think of anything else to do. He thought that, perhaps, reading a book may do him some good. So he got ready and ventured out. Jitendra had explained the way to him, so he didn't have any problem in locating the library. He went inside and started browsing. His eyes fell upon a book titled The Path to Peace. He picked it up and leafed through it. It had several chapters with interesting headings. He found it appealing and sat down with it in a corner. He opened the first chapter and started reading.

THE SEARCH FOR HAPPINESS IN THE ROOTS OF UNHAPPINESS

You encounter many problems in your life and become unhappy, but have you ever explored your unhappiness? Have you ever tried to find the root cause of your suffering? If you want to permanently free yourself from suffering, you need to reach the root of your unhappiness. You have to become an investigator of the inner truth. As an investigator of the inner truth, you can learn the art of being happy even in unhappy circumstances. To learn how to do this, you need to dive within and explore the depths of your mind. Gradually, you will become an expert at this and all the causes of your unhappiness will come to light and disappear.

What happens when a cause is brought to light? Its reality is exposed. Untruth disappears in the light, whereas the truth shines forth. That is how you know what is true. Whatever starts disappearing upon coming to light, had no existence to begin with. It was just an illusion which had been imprinted in your mind. You were either nurturing it in ignorance, or had ignored it in your pride and greed for material comfort.

All the unfortunate incidents in your life will keep recurring if you continue with your old outlook. And whenever these situations recur, they will make you unhappy. But when your eyes open to wisdom, all the causes of your suffering will come to light. All the events that used to make you miserable will start becoming the cause of your supreme happiness. The very people who used to hurt you will become your friends. When this starts happening to you, you will know that you have become an investigator of the inner truth. Otherwise, whenever something happens, you promptly stamp it as the truth under the influence of your old outlook. This habit of stamping prevents you from thinking in new ways. It closes your mind to any other possibility.

Hercules was shaken by what he read. 'How could this book be so apt?' he wondered. He continued reading.

WHAT IS THE MEANING OF STAMPING?

Stamping means branding something—a person, or a situation—according to your own perception. Say you are at work, and a colleague comes into your work area and doesn't look at you. He talks to someone else and leaves. It's such a simple event. There is nothing for you to feel perturbed about, but you feel indignant and hurt. You create a story and stamp it: 'He didn't even look at me—that means he doesn't like me.'

In his ignorance, man keeps creating such stories right from childhood. These stories vary according to his environment, his family's way of thinking and his upbringing. He lives his entire life based upon these make-believe stories.

In the above example, it could very well be you in place of the individual who did not look at you. If you are engrossed in some urgent or important work, it is likely that you do not pay attention to the people around you. That does not mean that you do not like them. But if someone else does the same to you, you immediately make up a story. This fallacy takes root in your mind and imprints unhappiness deep within you. Stamping is when you pass a judgement about an event, or a person, without thinking rationally, and without knowing the reality. When you give up this habit of stamping or, in other words, when you stop taking your immediate thoughts after an event as the gospel truth, then you will get new insight. You will be amazed by the fact that all the events which were the cause of your suffering have become the cause of your joy.

When you keep your prejudices aside and contemplate the event from a new perspective, then the same thing—that you had earlier stamped—reveals its entire existence. All the secrets tumble out and when the secrets are revealed, you won't remain displeased any more. When you do not know the secrets, you are disgruntled and spread sorrow. Reflect upon what you are spreading and how you look at each event. This investigation will reveal your nature to you.

Say you get shoved by someone, or someone you are waiting for is late, or someone doesn't take your call, steps on your foot while walking, ignores you, boasts in front of you—then your mind starts complaining. That is when you can thoroughly investigate your mind's habitual stamping and how its stories are just that—stories. After a period of investigation, you will reach a point where you will stop having negative feelings about these incidents. In order to experience this magic in your life, you need to dig deep into your mind. Then this investigation will become a joy. After your investigation, when you will look at the same incidents again, your root error will come to light. You will wait for such incidents to recur in order to witness your response to them. When you reach such a state, you will experience the bliss of freedom.

Hercules looked at his watch. He asked the librarian where he could buy the book. The librarian gave him the address of a bookstore in the local market. After asking for directions, Hercules found it. He then headed back to Jitendra's house. While walking, he couldn't help pondering over this newly acquired perspective and the importance of self-investigation. Until now, he had always trusted brawn over brains. But now his thought process had found a new direction. He read the book—about the three steps of investigating himself, about love, about handling children, about justice, about finding freedom in relationships—and felt empowered. He began to see the key to Jitendra's problems, as well as his own. He said to himself, 'Today onwards, I will team up with Jitendra to explore the solution to his troubles and unearth their root cause. This will definitely put an end to all his problems.' He was so engrossed in his thoughts that he didn't even realize when he reached Jitendra's house. After lunch, he went into the backyard and, lying in the lawn, he spent a couple of hours mulling over his new found wisdom.

Meanwhile, Jitendra continued pondering over his tribulations at home, while at work. He was eager to finish off the tasks so as to spend time in the evening with Hercules. He made it a point to leave office on time. It had been ages since he had come home in the evening.

The family had a quiet dinner. Jitendra then set out for a walk with Hercules.

The moment they left home, Jitendra started, 'Look, I'm perfect in all that I do. I keep everything in its assigned place. I never forget to complete all my chores. Even in the office, I work very well. But look at my children! All their things are always strewn around. Why can't they learn to be tidy like me? I just don't like untidy people.'

Hercules heard his rant silently, then told him about the first chapter of *The Path to Peace*. 'Now we will investigate and reach the root cause of your problem, after which we can find the solution,' he said.

Jitendra agreed unwillingly.

Hercules said, 'You keep all your things in their assigned places. You never forget to complete your chores. That is great. Now try to find those areas where you are unable to do this.'

Jitendra replied indignantly, 'I can't find any such areas!'

'Do you keep all your thoughts in their assigned places in the cupboard of your mind? Do you do everything according to your schedule? Do you pay regular attention to your health? Do you use your wealth correctly? Do you shoulder all your social responsibilities?'

This barrage of questions shook Jitendra. He started investigating within himself. He realized how careless he was regarding his physical health. He did not pay enough attention to exercise and nutrition. His mind was a bundle of unorganized thoughts. He did not use his money constructively. He avoided social commitments, despite regular requests from acquaintances—he thought they just added to his problems.

He agreed hesitantly, 'Now I can see some areas where I am a little disorganized.'

Hercules used this moment to drive home his point. 'You are careless about so many things. So, if your children are not perfect in a couple of areas, why must you get so angry? They are your mirror. They are showing you the areas where you commit similar mistakes.'

This was shocking news for Jitendra. For the first time, he understood his mistakes. He thought, 'If my wife and children are not behaving according to my expectations, then I need to calmly look inside myself and see whether I'm behaving according to my expectations at all times.'

He told Hercules, 'Until now, I used to think that I was an expert in all areas. But, after a little investigation, I've realized that I'm not perfect in my feelings, thoughts, speech and actions—in fact, they are not in sync at all. At the same time, I'm not perfect in the physical, mental, financial, social and spiritual areas either. Now I have understood that I should stop complaining about others because this is the biggest cause of my unhappiness.'

Hercules was happy with Jitendra's self-investigation. He said, 'We can find complete happiness in our lives only when our feelings, thoughts, words and actions are in sync. When they are not, we lead a fragmented life. This fragmented life becomes the reason for our unhappiness.'

With this new found wisdom, Jitendra could clearly see that, whenever his daughter used to get angry, he too would become angry thinking, 'Why is she angry?' After investigating within, he realized that his daughter's anger was a mirror showing him his own anger.

After a while, Jitendra hugged Hercules and said, 'Thanks to you, I have gained an insight into a new dimension of life. One by one, we will discuss all the issues that bother me and try to find their solutions.'

That night, Jitendra slept soundly after a long time. Hercules could not sleep. He wondered how a few words from the book could cause transformation. He attributed the transformation partly to the book and partly to faith. He decided to implement what the book said.

Jitendra felt very light the next morning. His perfectionism didn't bother him at all that day. Whenever he felt that somebody was not doing his tasks properly, instead of stamping him as imperfect, he reminded himself, 'I'm not perfect in many areas of my life either. I have no right to scold them. First, I must achieve perfection in all areas.'

He felt happy and at peace with himself all day long. Jagruti, the kids and Hercules too were glad at this change. In the evening, the children went out to play as usual. When they returned home, they started watching television instead of studying. This made Jitendra lose his newly acquired cool. He started shouting at them. He was already displeased with their performance in the examinations. They were not doing as well as he expected them to. The day the results were announced was always a day filled with tension. Jitendra used to scold them for their low grades, spoiling the atmosphere at home.

After dinner, as soon as Hercules and Jitendra went out for a walk, Jitendra started complaining, 'Look how hard I work to earn for my family, but my children can't even study properly. Both of my children scored very low in their unit tests, because of which their class teacher called me to school. I cannot tolerate such an insult. Now you tell me: How can I stay calm under these circumstances?'

Hercules asked, 'Have you forgotten yesterday's lesson?'

'That was a different issue,' replied Jitendra.

'I think it will be helpful if you can carry out a self-investigation on the basis of yesterday's insight. Your complaint today is that the children do not study. Now use this complaint as a mirror and ask yourself if *you* have completed *your* studies.'

'But I completed my studies a long time ago! I don't go to school any more. I have nothing to do with studies now.'

'It's true that you do not go to school any more, but the quest for truth and a happy life is your education now. Ask yourself, have you completed this education? In other words, have you contemplated upon all the aspects of your life where you are still incomplete?'

Hercules explained to Jitendra that children cannot be taught with harsh words. In fact, such words only make them feel as if they're letting their parents down. They feel as if they can't make their parents happy. This inadequacy gets imprinted on their tender minds and they start developing a sense of guilt. They become sad. They can't say anything to us, nor can they express their problems. In this way, because of our false beliefs regarding children and their education, we become miserable and make our children miserable too. We should use creative ways to help improve our children. We may not see instant results, but we do need to use a new way so that we can become happy first. We need to get rid of habits that cause suffering to others. When they see us happy, our children will become free from guilt and tension, and will begin to improve.

'This is a paradigm shift!' exclaimed Jitendra.

Hercules continued, 'Whenever their exam results are declared, children look at their parents' faces time and again to see their reaction. At such times, we need to reassure our children that our love for them does not depend upon whether they pass or fail. Only then will our children be able to progress. Otherwise they will remain fearful. And how can fearful children study well? How can fearful children recall all that they have studied during the exams? We need to release others from stress by becoming stress-free ourselves. If we are under stress, we end up spoiling everything.'

Hercules' arguments made sense to Jitendra. They helped relieve his stress.

Jitendra was very happy. In his heart, he felt a new love for his children. It was Sunday—a holiday—so everyone was at home. They spent the whole day joyfully. Jitendra behaved in a loving and wise manner. Not once did he reproach his children, so they were in high spirits. Jitendra was pleased to see the change in his children's behaviour—owing to his own behaviour, of course. He thanked Hercules from the bottom of his heart.

It was about 4 p.m. when Jagruti called out, 'Please come and have your tea.'

'Jagruti, haven't you made tea a bit early today?' asked Jitendra.

'Yes. I have to go to a friend's house to attend a function.'

'Fine, but prepare something special for dinner tonight and also fetch some sweets on your way back.'

Jagruti nodded and left.

When she returned later in the evening, Jitendra asked, 'What sweets have you brought?'

Jagruti said, 'Oh, I didn't get any. I am…'

'Do you ever remember to do anything?' shouted Jitendra.

Jagruti had decided to prepare the sweets at home, but Jitendra didn't give her a chance to complete her sentence. He just exploded without thinking. Jitendra believed that a woman should always obey her husband. Therefore, despite Jagruti making some delicious food for dinner, he remained angry. Hercules praised the food generously.

After the meal, Jagruti started doing the dishes, while Hercules and Jitendra left for their regular walk.

Immediately, Jitendra started complaining, 'Did you see, Hercules? Jagruti doesn't do anything the way I want. Not only that, she can't even learn anything. I feel terrible about it. Sometimes, when I can't take her phone call because of my busy schedule at work, she sends me a text message. When I read her messages, I feel embarrassed. Her English is so poor! She kills the language. Her broken English makes me feel ashamed of her. On returning home, I tell her about her mistakes. But she keeps repeating them again and again. It's been more than a year, but she hasn't made any progress whatsoever. I feel really bad about it.'

Hercules listened patiently. He had seen how Jitendra had behaved with Jagruti in the evening. Hercules thought that the best way to make him understand was to read out a story to him from *The Path to Peace*. They sat on a bench under a street light and Hercules started reading.

> There was a person who was always very unhappy and worried. One day, he approached his guru for help with his troubles. He said to the guru, 'I am fed up of my wife. She never behaves the way I want her to. Regular fights have almost killed the love between us. Is it possible to overcome this situation?'
>
> The guru answered with a question, 'Refresh your memory. Did you love her when you married her?'
>
> 'Of course I did,' the man replied.
>
> 'Then why are you having problems with her now? The thought that your wife will behave in such and such manner after marriage is nothing but fallacy—a story manufactured by your mind. Have you married the woman or have you married your

story about that woman? These things are so subtle that they don't come to light easily. You need to dig deeper to uncover the reality. Today you are so taken in by your imaginary story that you are unable to accept your life partner the way she is.'

The guru explained further saying, 'The problem is that man has become a tailor who wishes to fit his customer into the jacket he has tailored regardless of whether the customer is too thin or too fat for it! The tailor keeps waiting his entire lifetime for the customer to fit into his jacket so that he can become happy.

'Man suffers because he is adamant that each individual fit into his imaginary jacket. He wants everyone to walk, talk, eat, sleep, laugh and generally behave according to his desire. He wants them to dress according to his taste and be happy in his happiness. Just think and tell me: is this possible? Every person has a different body structure and different nature. Somebody may love shopping, but if his partner thinks of it as a waste of money, how can the partner remain happy?

'People build their beliefs and expectations around each relationship and consequently, suffer throughout their lives. A mother-in-law and a daughter-in-law look at each other through the lens of their beliefs. Initially, they both live together in harmony, but soon they start spinning their own stories about each other in their minds. Thus, the cycle of misery begins.

'Everyone expects the other person to change. You let your happiness depend upon whether or not the other person changes. You forget that when you had started the relationship, you had no stories about her. Gradually the stories started forming and the suffering began. Understand this truth and ask yourself in which relations you are attached to your stories.

'The irony is that even if someone does fit into your jacket, it doesn't keep you satisfied for long. You tailor another jacket and want that person to fit into this new jacket! In this way, you keep stitching new jackets for people to fit into, so much so that you don't spare even your neighbour, teacher, society or country! Sometimes, your near and dear ones try to fit themselves into your jacket, but you don't remain happy for long because you have developed the habit of stitching new jackets one after another.

'If you really want to be liberated from all suffering, you will have to let go of this habit of wanting people to be exactly the way you imagine. You will have to let go of your stubbornness and beliefs about relationships. You will have to accept people the way they are and love them. All this can be achieved only through understanding. No amount of coercion can help here.

'Are you ready to free yourself from all the false beliefs and stories that you have accumulated throughout your life? If you are, then give up all your complaints and start contemplating. Find out which relationships you have created unhappiness in. Investigate your own thoughts honestly. You have been living with your beliefs and stories for all these years, but they have not helped you in any way. So eliminate them and never let them control your life again.'

The man had been listening to the guru intently. He contemplated upon the words of the guru and understood that he wasn't in love with his wife. Instead, he was in love with his own story about his wife. As soon as he stopped loving his story he realized, 'My wife is just the way she used to be before marriage. I had fallen in love with her the way she was. So why am I creating a new story now and making us both suffer?'

Jitendra was taken aback on listening to this chapter. He found the analogy of the jacket very apt. He said to himself, 'This is exactly what I'm doing. How wrong I have been! It is wrong to get enraged and feel sad when your expectations are not met, because the expectations themselves are wrong to begin with. Today, I got angry with Jagruti for not getting the sweets. It never occurred to me that she may have thought of a better plan instead. The other day, when she finished her chores and went off to sleep, I got furious because she didn't stay on to chat with us. I didn't think about the stress that she was under due to my absence for four days, or that she may have been tired after working at home all day. I always look at situations through my perspective. Only last month I had promised to take her out for a movie and completely forgotten about it in the company of my friends. And when she was upset about it, I had become angry. The reality is, I fail to see my mistakes.

'Last week, my manager asked me to finalize the accounts but I chose to give priority to another job. I overlooked the assignment given by my manager. When I myself do not behave according to others'—and at times my own—expectations, I have no right to get angry when others don't behave according to mine. And I have the audacity to think of breaking close relationships over such issues? I am ashamed of myself.'

When he realized this, Jitendra said, 'Hercules, you have shown me the path that will lead me out of all my problems, worries and complaints. Now I will behave lovingly with all my family members. I won't lose my cool any more. I won't have too many expectations from others. If anything bothers me, I will start investigating within myself and seek out the areas in which I am making the same mistake. When I become complete, everything in my life will be complete.'

Hercules was pleased to hear this. He said, 'Why don't you perform an investigation right now? Let us talk about your complaint that

Jagruti does not improve upon her mistakes in the English language. Let us go back to the steps of investigating yourself as mentioned in the book. What do you think is the first step?'

'The first step is to see how I commit the same mistakes.'

'No, the first step is even more primary—to identify what exactly is bothering you.'

'In this case, my wife's poor English bothers me and she takes no steps to improve.'

'All right. Now, in the second step, ask yourself how you are committing the same mistake physically, mentally, socially, financially and spiritually. Let's look at the physical plane first. Investigate how you are poor in that aspect.'

'I do not exercise at all, nor do I take proper care of my diet. I can think of various other things.'

'Now, let's look at the mental plane. Find out how you are poor mentally.'

'I do not read books or other things that can sharpen my brain and stimulate my thinking. I can go on and on.'

'Now the social plane. How are you poor socially? Are you poor at any language yourself?'

'I am a living example of being poor socially because of anger. Also, I am very poor at the local dialect spoken here. I am good at English, but not at other languages, including German which we have to use for our German clients.'

'Fine. Now, financially. Are you poor at managing money?'

'No. Umm… Yes. I am not good at maintaining accounts.'

Good. You are honest. And now, find out how you are poor

spiritually.'

'I like to attend spiritual discourses. When I do that, my head clears. But I am not regular at all. And although there are so many things that I have learnt, I am poor at implementing them.'

'How do you feel now, Jitendra?' Hercules asked.

'I feel a bit better. I am no longer focussed on Jagruti. If she is poor at something, I am poor at many things too.'

'This is what investigating yourself does—it kills your ego and immediately helps you defocus from the faults of others. That is why it is so powerful in bringing about family harmony. Now that you feel happy, let us go to the third step. Look at reality again, while you are happy, and take action. What is the reality of the situation you are complaining about? And what action would you like to take?'

'The reality is that my wife sends me incorrect text messages. She makes grammatical mistakes.'

'That's it. Nothing beyond that. Is the reality that she is stupid and cannot understand anything? Is the reality that she does this deliberately?'

'No, that's not the case.'

'So, what action would you like to take now?'

'Nothing, for now. I will continue to be patient with her and continue to teach her English.'

Diving deep within, Jitendra discovered these pearls of wisdom. He frankly confessed to Hercules, 'There was a time when I liked Jagruti exactly the way she was. But now I have a story manufactured by my mind about how she should be. This has created all my problems. My inward search has made me realize that initially we accept everything but later on, we keep adding to a list of never-ending expectations. We forget the person whom we had accepted and loved. This truly does cause suffering.

'I promise you that the next time I read an incorrect text message written by Jagruti, I will smile and say, 'That's my wife!' This is whom I have chosen. Even if she never improves her English, it doesn't matter. It won't affect my happiness and I will not keep cribbing about it all my life. I won't worry about when she will learn how to write in proper English. Even if she does not, I won't let it affect me. If she does, that will be a bonus. My love will not be dependent on her English skills.'

Hercules smiled and said, 'You have far exceeded my expectations and learnt this process of self-investigation very quickly. Now, what about you complaining that she is forgetful?'

'I need to go through the three steps of investigation. First, find the exact cause of my unhappiness (the stamping). Second, analyse how I am myself forgetful physically, mentally, socially, financially and spiritually (the mirror). Third, see the reality happily and decide if any action needs to be taken (the communication).'

'That's great. You can complete your investigation by the time we get home. And take action happily,' said Hercules.

Both of them turned towards the home which would soon become a temple of love. As soon as they arrived, Jitendra went up gently to Jagruti and apologized for shouting at her earlier. He explained that he had lost his temper because she had forgotten to buy sweets. When Jagruti told him that she was going to prepare sweets at home, Jitendra felt ashamed. He promised her that he would, henceforth, keep his anger in check.

'That is okay. Just promise that you will do whatever Hercules is teaching you and come back to me lovingly every time,' Jagruti beseeched him tearfully.

'I promise I will try my very best. And I will request Hercules to teach you this technique as well. I am certain that there will come a time when we will not need to get angry at each other at all.'

When Jitendra was brushing his teeth before sleeping, he thought that maybe he could fall in love with his wife again. A little smile appeared on his face. But the very next moment, Jagruti's angry face danced before his eyes. He remembered all the cruel words she threw at him when he came home late from work. He remembered his suffering during those moments. He tried a lot to investigate himself in light of these incidents, but couldn't. He thought of asking Hercules about it to get rid of this miserable feeling forever.

In the other room, before turning in for the night, Hercules opened *The Path to Peace* and paid special attention to the chapter on marital relationships. He wanted to be prepared for any question from Jitendra.

'I am still unhappy about one thing,' said Jitendra to Hercules the next day. 'I tried to look at myself through that situation but couldn't succeed. Please guide me.'

'Tell me, what is bothering you?' Hercules asked.

'Whenever I get home late from work, Jagruti greets me with harsh words. She yells at me saying, "Is this the time to come home?" I can't control my anger at such times and I don't know how to react.

'When Jagruti asks you, "Is this the time to come home?" You should start investigating within yourself by using this sentence as your research material. Write down this sentence immediately.

The meaning of this sentence is that you spend a major portion of your time outside your "home". Here, the balanced condition of the mind is called "home". Jagruti says "Is this the time to come home?" only to remind you that you habitually stay out of the balanced condition of your mind, which means that you spend most of your time being upset, miserable and anxious. She may have uttered the sentence with some other intention, but you must always look at it in this particular manner. Until now, whenever you heard her say that line you thought, "She shouldn't have spoken like this. Perhaps she doesn't love me." This is the story you concoct. But from now on, this is a golden opportunity for you to unveil the false beliefs hidden inside you and bring to light the imaginary stories which only make you suffer. Just think objectively. What is hidden behind Jagruti's harsh words: hatred or love?'

Jitendra awkwardly replied, 'I know she does that out of love. But she insists that I come home on time!'

Hercules tried explaining, 'When the other person loves you and complains to you, it is not a major issue. Most people's problem is that the other person does not love them at all. From now on, think of how you can use Jagruti's words as research material for your internal investigation. This will help you bring balance in your life. You will also learn to manage your time well.

'When you don't look at your thoughts from all angles, they trouble you. But when you look at the other side of an issue, you understand that the other person is saying something out of love for you. If you feel hurt by Jagruti's words, tell her that being gentle will be more effective upon you. At the same time, also tell her, 'I have been making some blunders, but as I continue investigating within myself, I will improve.' In this way, if you bare your heart to her, she will understand you. The self-investigation will release the resistance from inside you and your behaviour will change. Jagruti too will not remain unaffected. She will begin to support you all the more.

'Prepare your plan of action and keep Jagruti involved. Tell her, 'This is the way I plan to work on myself, based on whatever you have said to me. I will be able to effect a change in some of these things immediately, while the rest will take some time.' If you communicate in this manner, then the same event will not create any resistance inside you subsequently, and your level of consciousness won't fall because you have correctly treated the sick thought which says she does not love you.

'Jagruti's role is to wake you up by pushing your buttons. When you start using her questions for self-exploration, then those questions will not make you miserable. Otherwise, even before reaching your home, the voices in your mind start saying that Jagruti is going to lash out again. Thus, your level of consciousness starts going down even before you reach home. The thoughts that you carry home with you produce the corresponding results. Now start thinking thoughts of love while you are on your way home. Think, "Jagruti loves me a lot. She will welcome me with love and a smile."

'Consider it divine grace that you are going to a house where you are continually being reminded, "Why do you reach your home—or, in other words, your inner centre—so late?" Take this admonition as a reminder and start your investigation. Ask yourself, "In which areas of my physical, mental, social, emotional and spiritual planes do I delay things? Do I take a lot of time to get back to my original state after a surge of emotion? Do I shed hundreds of tears before calming down?"

'After such an investigation, the tables will turn and you will say to yourself, "Is this the time to come home? Thank god this sentence has helped me explore myself. Now I shall reach every place on time.

Even at the level of emotions, I will stabilize at the earliest. I will not run after my thoughts but will centre myself as soon as possible."

'There are thousands of corners inside each of us that can provide us with priceless wisdom. We are unable to visit many of these corners on our own because they are beyond our thinking. We pay attention to them only when someone makes us aware of them. Jagruti is doing you a great service by drawing your attention to those unlit corners.'

'Is that so? I could have never imagined! You have brought a shift in my thinking. I am extremely grateful to you,' said Jitendra in a voice filled with admiration and gratitude.

Hercules kept reading *The Path to Peace* late into the night. This book presented solutions to many day-to-day problems using the medium of self-investigation. Hercules realized that this book was a great tool for changing many lives. He decided to buy a few more copies the very next day.

That night, Hercules kept thinking, 'Thanks to the blessings of the Goddess and the book, I have managed to save Jitendra's family-life by making him investigate himself. But what about my family-life? Am I not facing similar problems? I too had serious disputes with my wife and children, due to which they chose to live separately. I too expected a lot from people and when they couldn't meet those expectations, was displeased with them. Now I realize that, owing to my bad behaviour and self-righteousness, I was not coming up to others' expectations either. I neglected my family on many occasions. What right did I have to shout at them?'

Hercules accepted his mistakes and decided that, as soon as he was free from serving the priest, he would approach his wife and children and ask for their forgiveness. He also decided to promise them a life full of mutual love and respect. This firm resolve, coupled with his self-investigation, made him drop off and finally enjoy a good sleep after many days.

The next day was a holiday and everyone was home. A new atmosphere of joy and prosperity pervaded the house. Jitendra was so happy that he felt as though all the ten heads of the demon Ravana within him had been chopped off.

Hercules realized that his work was done. He had obeyed the priest and managed to solve Jitendra's household problems. He approached Jitendra and told him that it was time for him to leave. Suddenly, there was silence in the house.

Jitendra sighed, 'Today we are truly happy and you are saddening us by talking about leaving.' Jagruti too chimed in, 'You brought happiness into this house and helped repair our relationship. How will we solve our problems in future?'

Hercules presented a copy of *The Path to Peace* to them and said, 'You can find the solutions to all your future problems in this book.'

Hercules was amazed at his own capability. He had not only presented the tool of self-investigation to Jitendra and his family, but had armed himself with it. While counselling Jitendra, the answers to his own family problems had been revealed. He was pleased that his task of transforming twelve people's lives had gotten off to a great start with the blessings of the Goddess. He respectfully took leave of Jitendra and Jagruti and headed back to the temple.

'Ten more to go,' he thought, as he replayed the dream in which the Goddess had appeared. 'I have learnt so much about family harmony by pursuing the dream. Let me see where this journey takes me and what else I can learn.'

Three
The Second Task of Hercules: Clearing the Stables
—Investigating Work-Related Problems

After completing the evening rituals and prayers, the priest closed the doors of the temple and started walking towards his quarters. At that moment, he saw Hercules walking up the hillock towards him. The priest was taken aback. 'How could he come back so soon? Has he run away from Jitendra's house without solving his problems?' he wondered.

He faked a welcoming expression and inquired, 'How did you return so fast? What's the matter?'

'I've been able to solve Jitendra's family problems,' answered Hercules cheerfully and told the priest the entire story.

The priest was astounded. Full of curiosity, he asked, 'How could you manage such a feat?'

'Through the blessings of the Goddess,' Hercules replied humbly.

The priest felt belittled. He was the priest of the temple, yet the Goddess had never blessed him in this way. But Hercules had been showered with special grace. Then he realized that he had never prayed honestly from the bottom of his heart. He was just pretending to be a priest. Besides, he had other pressing problems to deal with.

He thought, 'Now that Hercules is here again, how will I run my business? I must find some new excuse soon to send him far away.' Outwardly, he smiled and said, 'Well done. You must be tired. You should go and rest now.'

Having listened to Hercules' unique way of solving family problems through self-investigation, the priest realized that he was no ordinary man. He thought that perhaps Hercules had some inner power that helped him face every problem with ease. On one hand, his harsh behaviour towards Hercules softened. On the other, he kept wondering how to get rid of him.

The next day, the priest's sister Maya approached him. She started complaining about her husband saying, 'Mahesh has not been happy with his job for a long time. But now he has stopped going to work altogether. I have to run the household with two children, pay their school fees and deal with a depressed Mahesh. How can I handle all these responsibilities?' She broke down and started sobbing. She pleaded with him to come home with her immediately and find a solution.

The priest tried to console Maya and said, 'I shall definitely think of something in a day or two.' Suddenly, he got an idea: Why not send Hercules? He felt as though the Goddess had blessed him with this idea. Hercules may, in fact, be able to solve Maya's problems. And even if he wasn't successful, he would at least be out of his hair. He told Maya, 'I have too many responsibilities here. So I can't come myself. But I can send a very competent disciple named Hercules immediately to help solve your problems.' He assured her, 'The Goddess has blessed Hercules. He has special powers with which he can easily solve all your problems.'

After talking to his sister, the priest called Hercules and instructed him, 'Now I'm going to assign another job to you. I am certain that you'll be able to do it well. My sister Maya just called. She was crying. Her husband Mahesh is not interested in his job and has stopped going to work. This worries her a great deal. You have to go to their house to help solve their problems. You can leave after lunch.'

'Certainly! Your servant is ready to serve you,' replied Hercules with great zeal. The priest gave him Maya's address and bade him goodbye.

Hercules thought, 'What special grace has descended upon me! The Goddess sends me to solve only those problems that reflect my own issues! I shall manage to investigate my own business troubles through this task.'

When Hercules reached Maya's house, he found Mahesh slumped in a couch, lost in thought. Maya too looked tense. Hercules introduced himself. Maya felt reassured by the fact that her brother had sent someone to help them. Hercules tried to lighten the atmosphere by some light-hearted banter, but Mahesh didn't say a word.

Hercules comforted Maya by saying, 'Be patient. Circumstances in life keep changing. Every night is followed by day. Do not worry. We shall try our best to bring Mahesh out of this condition. The Goddess will make everything all right. Always remember that each problem, each suffering, is an opportunity in disguise.'

Hercules kept explaining things and reassuring Maya and Mahesh day after day. Even though Mahesh had not yet opened up to him, Hercules persisted without losing his cool. He started pulling him out of the house on the pretext of small errands or a stroll. After a few days, Mahesh became more comfortable and started speaking a little about his workplace. Then one fine day, he opened up completely and related all his problems to Hercules, in front of Maya.

He said, 'I'm fed up of the environment in my office. I don't feel like going to work. Every day I have to face one problem or another. Mental tension demoralizes me and my mind gets filled with all sorts of negative thoughts. Even the thought of my office makes me feel sick in the stomach. So I've stayed away from work for the past three months. About a week ago, I convinced myself to get ready for work, but then I felt that I wouldn't be able to face the situation there. The very thought gave me palpitations and I developed a high fever due to the anxiety. I had to extend my sick leave further.'

'But what kind of problems do you face in the office?' Hercules asked.

'I face a lot of problems there. My colleagues ignore me completely. They don't treat me with respect. Whenever I look at them, they pretend to be busy with their work. I feel very bad and neglected. Recently, one of my colleagues got a promotion. He shared this good news with the entire staff—except me. I felt very hurt by his oversight.' There was tension in the air. After a pause, he continued, 'That's not all. My boss always rebukes me. He tries to put me down in front of others. All the challenging and creative assignments are given to other employees, even if they are junior to me. I have to be content with boring routine work. On top of that, the boss praises others in front of me and criticizes me in front of them. What more can I tell you? People ignore me to such an extent that, if I join their group during lunch or tea, all conversations stop suddenly. I feel as if I'm the most awful and worthless person on the face of the earth.'

Maya couldn't take it any more. She started weeping uncontrollably and implored Hercules, 'Brother, please say something. What is the solution to these problems?'

Hercules told Mahesh, 'I have a great tool called self-investigation. This tool can solve all your problems. Are you willing to use it?'

'Of course! But tell me how this tool will help me,' Mahesh inquired.

'For that, you will need to investigate within yourself.'

'What do you mean by that and what exactly do I have to do?'

'Whatever problems you have enumerated, we will investigate them. You said that people ignore you. Now you have to contemplate upon the question: When do I ignore other people?'

Mahesh felt confused initially, but then he reflected upon this aspect. Soon many facets of his behaviour became evident to him. He realized that, in his ignorance, he too neglected people in many instances. Maya's regular complaint was that Mahesh ignored her completely. He was not too comfortable with his relatives either and often neglected them. At the same time, he often neglected his work and his various duties. Yet when people neglected him he felt terrible!

Mahesh told Hercules all this. Hercules felt happy and hopeful. He asked Mahesh, 'What about your own self? In which areas do you neglect your own self? Think about it.'

'Oh, yes! I've never given this a thought. I neglect my physical health. I know that a morning walk is good for health but I keep postponing it. I know what to do but I don't do it.' Mahesh found many other areas where he was ignoring himself. This investigation made him realize that, before complaining about others neglecting him, he should first stop neglecting himself and others. He suddenly felt his complaints recede. He decided, 'From now on, I will pay attention to myself and others. I'll be attentive at work and towards all my other duties. When my behaviour changes, perhaps people will change too and stop neglecting me.'

The incident of his colleague's promotion had convinced Mahesh that his colleague didn't like him. His inner investigation made him realize that he too often forgot to tell some important things to Maya. That didn't mean he didn't like her. Such errors happen sometimes. This new understanding helped Mahesh let go of his erroneous belief that his colleague disliked him. Mahesh thought, 'I should be happy that my colleague has been promoted. My life will become more joyful if I start participating in others' joys.'

Mahesh investigated this incident from one more perspective. He thought, 'If my colleague has hidden something from me, I must look at my own life and find out how I hide things from others and from my own self.' This brought out some other hidden facts. He never told his parents that, sometimes, he went to the bar with his friends. Many a time, he had hidden good news from his relatives. For example, he didn't tell them that he had bought a new computer and music system. Often he hid things from himself as well. Instead of accepting that he was lazy and poor at time management, he often excused himself from helping his children with their homework saying he didn't have time. He had never admitted this truth, even to himself.

Mahesh felt lighter after listening to all the answers that his investigation threw up. He felt happy inside.

Hercules said, 'Now that you've decided to stop deceiving yourself, you will progress very quickly. Tell me, what else bothers you?'

Mahesh thought for a while and said, 'I think all my issues have been resolved!'

'All right. You may not remember everything at once but, as soon as you remember something, just write it down in your diary. Whenever you find the time, investigate that topic in writing as well.'

Mahesh was happy for a day or two, but then he began to remember the other problems that he used to face. As instructed by Hercules, he wrote down all the issues in his diary and explored them. After some days, he placed his diary in front of Hercules and said, 'I have written down all my problems and investigated them in writing. I want to share my insights with you.'

'That's fabulous! Please go ahead,' said Hercules.

Mahesh began reading from his diary, 'My subordinates do not obey me. They don't do their work properly and on time. They do not respect me.' He then read out his investigation. 'I too do not obey my superiors. Instead of doing the work assigned by them, I follow my own schedule at my own leisure. Thus, I disrespect them. Even at home, I do not really respect my parents and elders. I never make the effort to do any task to the best of my ability. Then what right do I have to get angry with my subordinates' behaviour?'

Hercules offered further guidance. 'Now think how many times, even after getting insights from within, do you actually follow them? Do you think in the right manner at the right time? Do you respect yourself?'

'You're absolutely right. Generally, I suffer from an inferiority complex. I consider myself inferior to others. If I don't respect myself, how can I expect others to respect me? I must first acquire self-respect,' said Mahesh.

He then turned to the next page of his diary and read out his second investigation. 'My complaint was that my colleagues get faster promotions and better increments than I do. After inquiring within, I realized that it is just my belief, a story I have woven. The level of work and the responsibilities of my colleagues are different. Their work is more creative and important. It is but natural that the management would want to encourage them and retain them in the company. The company knows how to do its business. I too do not behave equally with my two children. Depending upon the need and the situation, I give one of them more encouragement than the other. Also, every person is entrusted with the responsibility that he is capable of handling and it is on that basis that he receives benefits.

'If I had gotten a promotion, would I have turned to contemplating upon these truths? Perhaps nature is helping me contemplate and achieve true success through self-development. But how am I reacting to this help? It's time I grabbed it with both hands and made true progress.'

'You've got it, Mahesh!' said Hercules, delighted.

Mahesh's next grievance was, 'Others are given the opportunity to travel abroad, not me.'

During the course of his investigation he asked himself questions like, 'Am I completely trained for overseas projects? Have I ever made my potential known to my superiors? Am I capable of taking important decisions? Those who possess all these qualities get the opportunity to go abroad and work there.' His investigation also made him realize that 'whenever the company proposed to send me on site for some important job, I declined the offer citing one problem or another. Actually, I was scared of shouldering the added responsibility. I also wanted to avoid the challenges that such assignments posed. Perhaps I was not confident about carrying out the job. Under such circumstances, how could I be selected for overseas assignments and special responsibilities? When I start doing my work enthusiastically, cheerfully, expertly, punctually and without any expectations, I will automatically be selected for special tasks.'

Hercules was thrilled with Mahesh's investigation. He said, 'When you become worthy of something, it finds you on its own. This is an infallible law of nature. You need to enhance your worthiness and capability, so keep working on improving yourself in every way.'

'I certainly will,' said Mahesh and continued reading from his diary. 'In a meeting, no one pays attention to my suggestions. My recommendations are ignored.' A deeper search revealed: 'When my colleagues or subordinates offer me some suggestions, I don't take them seriously either. So much so that, even when my wife or children try to tell me something I completely veto their ideas. I do not think deeply about issues in the meetings. I just offer suggestions for the sake of appearing involved. My thoughts are not well-directed, nor do I have the courage of conviction. I often go on a tangent and say things that are not relevant. So who will take me seriously? Who will listen to me? I'm determined to first correct all my flaws. Now I do not harbour any ill-will against anyone. I have no complaints.'

Hercules and Maya, who had been listening silently until now, were astonished at this change.

Thus, under Hercules' guidance, Mahesh attained an understanding of how to investigate his suffering. He was happy now. He had found a new way of thinking. All the factors that had seemed intolerable to him now became a cause for happiness. His thoughts had received a new direction. He realized that his bitter experiences at the office had proven to be instrumental in transforming his life. He felt the divine hand in this drama. He knew that he was blessed to be receiving this guidance from Hercules. Unpleasant events had occurred in his life in order to help him. But for them, he would never have thought of digging within. He would never have moved towards inner peace and joy. Now he was confident of solving any difficult situation without inventing stories and inviting the resultant suffering. Hercules had helped Mahesh free himself from all his false beliefs and stories. His inner exploration had solved all his work-related problems and relieved him of suffering. His conviction that he would never be able to solve his problems, that he would fail, came to light after self-investigation and he was able to overcome it. After ages, a smile returned to his lips.

At dinnertime, when he expressed his desire to resume work the very next day, Maya couldn't hide her happiness. On one hand, Mahesh was excited about going back to work. On the other, he wasn't too sure that the office politics and work pressure would not make him miserable once again. He told Hercules his doubts.

'You have just come out of your depression, so it's natural for you to feel this way. But now you are equipped with the sword of self-investigation. Use it! Just go to the office with an open mind and behave nicely with everyone. Also remember that you are not supposed to look at how the other person is wrong. You only have to see how he is right. Whatever you pay attention to starts becoming a part of you, so pay attention to others' good qualities. Nevertheless, if you encounter some difficulty tomorrow, we shall investigate it at night,' Hercules counselled Mahesh.

The next day Mahesh left for the office with a twinge of nervousness. He had been absent for a long time and people welcomed him and inquired about his health with unexpected warmth. Mahesh was touched by their behaviour. When his manager asked him about his well-being, he frankly told him everything about his depression, his false beliefs and his self-investigation under Hercules' guidance. The manager was impressed by this turnaround and expressed his desire to meet Hercules.

As soon as Mahesh reached home in the evening, he told Hercules and Maya about all that had happened at the office with great zest. He also said that his manager and some colleagues were keen to meet Hercules. It was decided that Mahesh would bring these people home after work the next day. They would be able to interact with Hercules over tea and refreshments.

The next evening, when they came to Mahesh's home, they were all very impressed with Hercules and his tool of self-investigation. Mahesh's manager thanked Hercules and assured Mahesh that he would do everything to improve the environment at work, making it more friendly and cheerful. With this assurance, he and the others took leave of Mahesh and Hercules.

Within a few days it became clear that Mahesh was happy to get back to work. He was working with renewed vigour and confidence. Maya felt as if she'd found a treasure-house of happiness. She told Hercules, 'Your guidance has transformed Mahesh. I offer my heartfelt gratitude to you. Now I understand how we tend to get stuck in our make-believe stories and harm ourselves.'

Hercules remembered some pages from *The Path to Peace*. He told Mahesh and Maya, 'It's because of his habit of remaining unhappy that man makes a lot of mistakes. Therefore, it is imperative for us to always remain happy and make a habit of it, or at least try to become happy when we are unhappy. I'll give you a book. Please read it together.' Saying so, he gave them the book and left for a walk.

'The sooner the better,' said Maya and started reading it aloud, with Mahesh listening attentively.

WHEN TO STAY HAPPY

> If someone asks you, 'For how much time in a day would you like to be happy?' You will answer, 'All the time!' And if the question is, 'For how much time can you remain happy in a day?' You will answer, 'Well, I can remain happy for at least this amount of time.' Now the next question will be, 'But what is

the minimum amount of time that you should remain happy? And when and why should you remain happy for that amount of time?' What answer will you give to this question? And what answer will emerge after investigating within?

Mahesh said, 'What could the answer be?'

Maya said, 'Let me read what's written.'

> At first, people will say that we should remain happy for at least such and such a period of time in a day, during such and such events, and so on. But after investigating, they will realize that the answer is: 'It is important to stay happy at least during those times when there is unhappiness.' Whenever you come across unhappiness, start being happy. If you can do this, then everything will start improving because only in happiness can you see everything clearly—in unhappiness you cannot.

> Say you're travelling in a car. Your car's windscreen is covered with dust and you cannot see clearly. Suddenly the car slows down and you wonder, 'Perhaps there's a speed-breaker that's slowing the car down. And why is the person behind me honking? Can't he understand?' This is how you begin thinking. But when, suddenly your car comes to a halt, you realize that it has gotten entangled in the bushes.

> If your car's windscreen was clear, you could have seen that the car had slowed down not because of a speed-breaker but because of the bushes, and that the person behind you was honking to warn you. He wanted to help. Thus, when you see everything clearly, there is no need for thinking about any thing else. It's only when you cannot see well, you start thinking unnecessarily.

'This is so true. You stopped seeing even normal things because you were too entangled in your own make-believe story about office problems. In your misery, you kept thinking unnecessarily. Isn't that so?' Maya felt she could now tease Mahesh a bit.

'You're right, dear. Let's hear what's next,' Mahesh replied.

> Once you begin to see clearly, your unnecessary thinking ceases. When you start seeing your own life clearly with this understanding, your investigation is complete. Before you start investigating, put a stop to all the stamping and the constant chattering of your mind. Then carry out the investigation. You will be able to catch the essence of the teaching: 'It is essential to stay happy at least during those times when there is unhappiness.'

> Such insights come to you when you get connected with the source—your original natural state, the experience of the Self. Only through contemplation can you get connected with your original natural state. In this state, your ignorance leaves you and you see everything clearly. Everyone appears in their true state. That is why you begin to like everyone. Then people ask you with great surprise, 'How come you are so happy in this situation?' And you answer, 'Why shouldn't I be happy? Everything is perfect in my life. What is there to be unhappy about?'

'Wow! Everything has been explained so beautifully. We have experienced this too. This is our story,' Maya said excitedly. Mahesh agreed with her. Maya continued to read.

> Come, let us understand our story through an analogy. This imaginary story will help you understand things clearly.

> There is a tradition in a village according to which, when a child becomes two or two-and-a-half years old, a special ceremony is

held in which he is made to wear a pair of red goggles. The whole world looks different through these goggles. All the villagers in that village wear red goggles. These are no ordinary eyeglasses. The frame is made from a special wood and sutured around the eyes so that the goggles stay in place at all times. Now, as the child grows up, the world looks to him as it looks to the elders.

'That's right. A child is simple and innocent until he is about two-and-a-half years old. Later, we start filling our wrong beliefs in his mind,' said Mahesh, understanding the analogy immediately.

'It's true,' agreed Maya. 'Let us read further.'

You can imagine how much the villagers miss in their lives. You can understand that what the villagers see is not reality, but an illusion.

Once, it so happens that the goggles of one of the village boys comes off for a short while. Perhaps the rituals were not conducted properly or the suturing was not adequate. The goggles dislodge from its place for a short while due to a jolt and fall back in place once again. Even though this happens for a very short while, during that time the boy sees the world as it is. From that day onwards, everything changes for him and his inner quest begins.

Some people begin their existential search using the wrong tools, such as drugs, liquor, etc. Under the influence of intoxicants, the world looks different to them. They want to go into that experience again and again. This keeps them hooked to that intoxicant. Each time, they need a bigger dose to get the same experience. The reality is that these intoxicants destroy your life. How can something destructive be helpful in your inner quest? Inner investigation needs positive thinking and constructive tools.

'Hercules has removed my red goggles and saved me from such destructive habits,' said Mahesh with genuine gratefulness.

Maya too felt grateful. She then handed over the book to Mahesh and said, 'Now it's your turn to read.' Mahesh began:

> Now this boy keeps pondering about what he saw in that moment when his glasses had slipped. New thoughts, which had never appeared before, begin to rise in his mind—just like someone who attends a spiritual discourse finds his false beliefs slipping off after listening to the guru and begins to look at things from a new perspective. He feels like investigating this phenomenon. He starts looking at life's events in a different manner.
>
> Once in a while, a wandering ascetic—whom the villagers call a lunatic—is seen in this village. Whenever he enters the village, he is chased away because he does not don the mandatory red goggles. The villagers feel that their children will be scared of this man. They also fear that this man may encourage new thoughts in their children. Therefore, they do not allow the ascetic to stay in the village. That is why he lives among ruins outside the village. This boy looks at the ascetic and thinks, 'Why is he not wearing goggles like the rest of us? Why are his eyes different from the rest?'
>
> One day, he goes to the ruins to meet the ascetic and is astonished. He asks, 'Why don't you wear clothes?' The weird ascetic quietly replies, 'Because at first we don the clothes. But later on, the clothes don us.' The boy fails to understand this answer. He asks another question, 'Why are your eyes red?' The ascetic gives a mysterious smile and says, 'Because there is something stuck in your eyes.' The boy finds these answers

illogical. He cannot understand a thing. Still, he cannot contain his curiosity and asks another question, 'Why do you live in these ruins?' The ascetic laughs loudly and replies, 'These are not ruins but a palace.'

These bizarre answers make the boy's head spin. He is convinced that this ascetic is completely insane. But his heart feels like meeting him time and again.

After a few days, he pays another visit and says, 'Whatever you told me the other day is beyond my understanding. Clothes keep us from feeling cold, but you tell me that the clothes wear us. Pray tell me the meaning of your words.'

The insane ascetic says, 'Has the cold decreased just because you have worn warm clothes? The weather is what it is.'

'That's right,' the boy thinks for a while and replies. He feels that there is some truth hidden in the insane ascetic's words.

Now he makes frequent visits to the ruins. Slowly, he begins to understand the ascetic's words. He starts doubting his red goggles. He thinks, 'This ascetic keeps telling me to change my outlook. Perhaps the problem lies in my faulty outlook.' Only when that boy starts doubting his goggles (of ignorance) does he become ready to take them off and look at the world without them. As soon as he removes them, everything is clearly visible to him. He sees that the ascetic is wearing red-coloured clothes and his eyes are not red. He realizes, 'My red glasses were fooling me. My faulty vision was preventing me from seeing the reality. Now I understand what the ascetic meant when he said there was something stuck in my eyes.'

Now he considers the ascetic his guru. The guru did not tell him at the beginning that his goggles were faulty. If he had told him right at the beginning, the boy would never have agreed. He may have even gotten upset, and an upset person can never understand the truth. Only a happy person can. Therefore, the guru indirectly told him that there was something stuck in his eyes.

'Even in my case, Hercules gradually told me things and made me analyse where I was going wrong,' said Mahesh.

'Absolutely! No amount of gratitude we offer him is enough. Let us understand the rest of the story,' said Maya.

> As he continues to visit the guru, the boy realizes that his guru's abode is indeed a palace. He could not see all the parts and colours of the palace earlier because of his goggles. Everything there is whole and colourful. He understands the secret of his guru's constant joy. Often, people think that a happy and cheerful person is insane. This ascetic too was living a constantly happy life in the 'ruins' and, therefore, the villagers took him to be insane.
>
> Next, the boy understands the meaning of the sentence: 'Our clothes wear us.' It means that our body is our garment. First, we wear this garment. Then, this garment wears us. This implies that we live our lives thinking of ourselves as a body, and interact with others considering them to be bodies as well. The Self, the truth, the self-witness remains hidden behind the body.
>
> When the boy takes off his glasses, he is shocked at the way the villagers are living their lives. They cannot see the way they should. After learning the truth, the boy feels like running to the village and asking everyone to throw off their goggles. He thinks, 'If the villagers do this, they will see a new, better and beautiful world. But they will not believe me. They will think

that I'm crazy. But I don't care if they believe me or not. I must begin my work immediately.'

'I have already started this work by inviting people to meet Hercules,' beamed Mahesh.

'Yes, that's great! Now let us read the meaning of this story,' said Maya.

> Each analogy has some pointers. These pointers lead you to the truth. Let us understand the various pointers in this analogy.
>
> Village: World
>
> Red goggles: False beliefs
>
> Boy: Seeker
>
> Insane ascetic: Self-realized guru
>
> Something in the eye: Wrong thinking
>
> Clothes: Body
>
> Ruins: A state wherein feelings, thoughts, words and actions run in different directions
>
> Palace: Tejasthan, the state of being stabilized in the Self

Let us understand this analogy in detail and compare it with our own life.

The villagers did not allow the insane ascetic to live in their village because they were scared of him. They did not want any child in the village to be inspired by him and think of removing the red goggles.

When the boy contemplated upon the answers given by the ascetic, some things became clear to him. Similarly, when you take a few sentences of the Truth and begin to reflect upon them, you can get profound insight.

'How true! We have been leading our lives this way for so long because of societal pressure,' sighed Maya. Mahesh concurred with her. Maya asked him to read further.

> Only when someone gives up his habit of stamping (or, in other words, stops wearing the red goggles), can he move forward and investigate within himself. Otherwise, the investigation comes to a complete halt. Just as the boy realized that it was because of his red goggles that he couldn't see the ascetic's red clothes and thought that his eyes were red, you too will gradually realize that all the shortcomings you see in others are actually your own. These things will become clear to you only after you use the tool of inner investigation. You will then say,

> 'I need a mirror to know myself. If another person has become a mirror for me, it is because of divine grace.'

> For example, you may crib that a person is a shirker. But when you do some soul-searching, you will realize that you too shirk work on many occasions. Every person likes or dislikes some work according to his preferences. The work another person finds difficult may be easy for you. That is why you think he is an idler while you consider yourself to be efficient. But there are some things that you cannot do. Do you consider yourself a shirker in those situations? When you begin to dig deep within, you will find many such things that you cannot do. Is it right, then, to stamp someone as a shirker?

> During your inner investigation, you have to look for all such areas where you shirk work. The other person is just your mirror. Once he shows you your weakness, his role is over. He has done his job—now your job begins. Don't keep saying,

'When will he improve?' Start applying makeup to yourself when you see your blemishes in the mirror! In other words, stop pointing out faults in others and start improving yourself. Once you start applying makeup on yourself, the world will not look the same. It will look more beautiful. You will be able to forgive people without complaining about them. The day you find everyone beautiful and start liking everyone will be the day you have become a good and beautiful person. Whatever you see in the world is just telling you about yourself. Otherwise how will you know yourself? The eye needs a mirror to look at itself. Similarly, man needs a mirror, in the form of relations and events, to see the faults within him.

'This means that our investigation should continue until we find everyone beautiful,' said Maya with a spark in her eyes.

'Yes. This is an exceptional chapter worth contemplating upon. Let us complete it first. We shall then reflect upon it in depth,' said Mahesh and continued reading.

> Man needs to investigate within himself in order to know himself. When he is cleansed of all his faults and his ego dissolves, he becomes stabilized in the ultimate truth. The dissolving of the ego is difficult because he is entangled in his various beliefs. If you want to wash your clothes with soap, you need to first remove the soap from its wrapper. Likewise, if man wants to achieve self-realization, he will have to be removed from his wrapper of miseries. Then he will be able to see everything clearly. He will realize that whatever he is seeing in the other person and whatever is bothering him is actually his own reflection.
>
> You will be able to provide proof of contemplation after deep investigation. What is proof of contemplation? When you can

explain how your contemplation on painful events ended your pain, that is your proof of contemplation. You need to annihilate each and every painful incident in your life and provide yourself with the proof of contemplation. In other words, you need to investigate deep within yourself and encounter the truth about yourself.

After reading through this chapter, Mahesh and Maya fell silent for a while. Even though Mahesh had been investigating his office problems with help from Hercules, he and Maya had only now understood the extent to which inner investigation should be carried out. They were stunned at the enormous possibilities that could open up.

In the evening, they both were eager to share their thoughts with Hercules. Mahesh began by saying, 'I was depressed due to the behaviour of the people in my office. I had entangled myself in my own beliefs and had a great number of expectations from others. I could finally rid myself of my false beliefs and depression because you taught me to use the tool of inner investigation. But now, after reading this particular chapter of the book, I realize that we need to carry out this investigation in all aspects of our lives so that we don't get stuck in any issue concerning any individual or incident.'

Maya totally agreed.

Mahesh carried on, 'This investigation helped me change my attitude towards my colleagues. But I was still afraid. What if some unpleasant incident occurred that I hadn't investigated? Or what if someone else treated me badly? What would I do then? But now, after reading this chapter, I feel confident about exploring every dimension of my life. I will bring each of my hidden beliefs to light and free myself from them. I'm sure I will not suffer any more.'

Maya said, 'When Mahesh gave up work and sat at home, my mind said, "It's all over now," and I was completely distraught. If I had stayed happy at that time, I would have had a clear view of things and I could have offered solace to Mahesh. He could have recovered faster with my help. Instead of being depressed by this incident, I should have used it as a mirror and improved my conduct.'

Mahesh and Maya both agreed that they needed a master in their life like the guru in the book. They expressed their desire to follow the teachings given in the book until they found a living master.

They were leading a happy life now—their major problems had been resolved. Hercules said, 'My job is complete. Now I must head back.' Mahesh and Maya did not feel like letting him go and requested him to stay for a few days more.

At night, Hercules was sitting alone on the terrace of the house. He was lost in thoughts of his past. 'Just like Mahesh, I used to be unhappy in my showroom. How foolish I have been, how many blunders and follies I have committed! I wish I'd received this guidance at that time—then I wouldn't have had to run away in this manner.' Then he realized the grace of god. How he saw the Goddess, how he came to the priest, how he got hold of *The Path to Peace* when he needed to solve people's problems. He couldn't sleep. He kept recalling his dream and the vision in which the Goddess had asked him to transform twelve people's lives.

A shudder ran down his spine when he realized that all the problems he'd helped solve until now were his own problems as well. All the problems Mahesh was facing with his manager and colleagues were similar to the problems that he'd created for his business partner and subordinates. His behaviour was responsible for their lack of support. Hercules had come face-to-face with himself. He decided to give up his habit of trying to control others and promised himself that he would create a joyful atmosphere in his showroom. This thought made him feel lighter. He realized that his search for the answers to his familial and business problems was over.

His inner being filled with gratefulness to the Goddess who had guided him to *The Path to Peace* and also provided him with the right words at the right time to help Mahesh. His eyes welled up thinking about the transformation that Mahesh had experienced. Before going to sleep, he decided not to stay there any longer. He wanted to meet the priest and find out what his next task was so that he could change ten more lives as soon as possible.

The following evening, he took leave from Mahesh and Maya and headed for the temple.

Four
The Third Task of Hercules: Slaying the Birds—Investigating Everything that is Unjust and Unfair

The night had deepened. His worries prevented the priest from falling asleep. Ever since Hercules had appeared in his life, his drug trafficking had almost come to a standstill. He had many small suppliers but his main supplier was Bhaiji, the owner of a beach resort. There had been a delay in the shipment from Bhaiji and the priest was worried that it would not reach him before Hercules' return. He called up Bhaiji and apprised him of his problem.

Bhaiji said, 'Why don't you send Hercules over to me? I'll keep him at my resort under some pretext until your goods are delivered. Only after the coast is clear will I let him leave this place.'

The priest liked Bhaiji's suggestion. 'Wonderful! As soon as Hercules returns from Maya's home, I will send him to you.'

The moment he put the phone down, it rang. Maya was on the line. She told her brother everything, starting from the time Hercules entered her home. She was full of praise for Hercules and gave him full credit for Mahesh's transformation. She also informed him that Hercules had left their home that evening and would reach the temple the next morning.

In the morning, when the priest completed his chores and went to the temple for the morning prayers, he found Hercules waiting for him. Looking bright and happy, he bowed and greeted the priest. For the first time, the priest felt something positive for Hercules. After all, he had helped his sister get rid of her troubles. He blessed Hercules generously. Both sat on a bench and started talking.

'Yesterday Maya informed me that you were coming. She also told me about the creative manner in which you solved Mahesh's problems. She is very happy that Mahesh has started working again. She has expressed her sincere gratitude to you,' said the priest.

'All this was possible because of the blessings of the Goddess,' replied Hercules with modesty. 'How else would I have managed?'

Blessings of the Goddess! The words pierced the priest's heart and filled it with envy once again. He wondered how everything that Hercules undertook was completed successfully with the blessings of the Goddess.

Hercules handed the priest a box of sweets and other gifts that Maya had sent. The priest accepted them happily and said, 'If I send you out for another important job tomorrow, would you be ready?'

Hercules hadn't even dreamt that his third task would be assigned to him so soon. He agreed at once.

Hercules' answer made the priest happy. At the same time, he thought, 'What is this guy made of? He doesn't complain, doesn't feel lazy or tired and doesn't make any excuses! He is always ready to obey all my orders. How committed he is towards his repentance, his penance!'

But he quickly shrugged off these good feelings for Hercules. He was only interested in keeping Hercules out of his way. He said, 'Rest for a while, now. We'll discuss this at night.'

'Fine,' said Hercules and retired to his room. As soon as he lay down on his bed, an acute attack of migraine gripped him. His head started throbbing and he moaned in agony. This headache was a big problem for him. He took out some balm from a box and rubbed it on his forehead. He worried about the problems awaiting him the next day. Suddenly, a voice within him said, 'All will be fine.' Now that he had decided to pay attention to his inner voice and take it as the final word, there was no room for doubt.

Though his head was still hurting, Hercules joined the priest for dinner. The priest told him, 'About 500 kilometres from here is a famous tourist spot called Mirama Beach. On that beach is a huge resort. Its owner Bhaiji is a friend of mine. He is a great devotee of the Goddess. He has been donating a lot of money for this temple. Go and stay with him for a few days.'

'But what will I do there?' Hercules asked.

'He is a big businessman. You will learn a lot of things while working with him. His company will be a great opportunity for you. You will stay there for as long as Bhaiji needs you.'

'Okay. Whatever you think is right for me. I shall leave in the morning.'

'You have just come from a long assignment. You can leave after a couple of days.'

'Whatever you say.'

Hercules rested and tried all possible remedies for his migraine. He felt much better in two days. On the third, he took the morning bus to his destination. Even though he was not certain about his duties there, he was happy to be going for his third task. He was also thrilled at the prospect of seeing the natural beauty of the lovely beach.

He remained engrossed in deep thought during the journey. These days, he used to feel a sense of satisfaction in his work. His conscience told him to share his understanding with as many people as possible. The bus continued its journey, stopping at some villages en route, halting for lunch and then resuming again. Hercules spent his time in silence, contemplation and prayer. Soon it was evening. The weather was perfect and the scene that unfolded before his eyes was enchanting. The sun was setting and the sky had turned golden red. Hercules looked out of his window for a long time, savouring each moment. His thoughts had come to a standstill.

The bus reached its destination at eight in the evening. Within ten minutes he was at the gates of the resort. He paid the taxi fare and walked towards his latest challenge.

He entered the premises and felt overwhelmed by the opulence of the resort. He went to the reception, introduced himself and asked to speak to Bhaiji. The receptionist asked him to wait in the lobby. Hercules sat on a luxurious sofa and started observing his surroundings. The resort was spread over a vast area. In fact, it was difficult to take it all in at once. It was decorated with palm trees, vibrant flowers, colourful fountains and shimmering lights. All means of entertainment were available to the guests.

After ten minutes, Hercules saw Bhaiji approaching. His appearance was commanding—business suit, dark complexion, stocky body and thick moustache. He introduced himself, shook hands and sat down on the adjacent chair. He was friendly and inquired about him and the priest. He then said, 'We'll meet again in the morning at ten. Till then you can have your dinner and relax in your room.'

In the morning, Hercules woke up to the chirping of birds. He freshened up and ate breakfast. Feeling fresh and wonderful, he walked up to the reception. He waited in the lobby for Bhaiji, who arrived at ten and sat near Hercules on the sofa.

'Good morning. Did you have a good night's sleep? How do you like this place?' Bhaiji asked.

'Good morning, Bhaiji. This is a beautiful place. It's very well maintained. But what exactly do I have to do here?' Hercules couldn't hide his eagerness.

'The resort's electronic maintenance manager has gone on leave for some days. Since you're an expert in the field, you can take care of all the electronic equipment in this resort. You have to manage the team of maintenance technicians and purchase new equipment as required. This is all your responsibility now.'

'It seems that the priest has given you a lot of information about me. All right, I'm ready to shoulder this responsibility.'

'The maintenance work can be done during the day. In the evening, we organize cultural and entertainment programmes for the tourists. If you have any such talent, you too will be given an opportunity to exhibit it. Spend a day or two watching all the activities here. If you need anything or face any problem, just let me know,' Bhaiji said and left with a smile.

The resort was not limited to the built-up area. Tourists were sprawled out under the open sky, enjoying various water sports or just looking at the waves. Some were sitting in the garden restaurant. Such close proximity to nature made even the elders behave like children. The weekends were especially busy. There were many small huts built on the beach. Each hut had a different attraction—magic show, puppet show and so on. At the far end, people enjoyed camel rides while some rode on carriages. Hercules was fascinated by his new environment. He spent a couple of days acclimatizing to the routine at the resort.

For the past couple of days, Hercules had been noticing a group of young men and women who would arrive at the resort late in the evening and leave only after the resort was closed for the day. They would spend their time talking and laughing, but there were moments of seriousness as well.

As usual, the group was busy discussing something this evening. Their expressions told Hercules that they were discussing something serious. Just then, a waiter approached them to take their order. Hercules saw that the group got into an argument with the waiter and started abusing him. 'This young generation needs to be guided out of darkness towards light,' he thought and approached them to sort out the matter. He made the waiter calm down.

After the waiter left, he asked them, 'I see you here almost every day. Can I join your group?'

All of them looked at each other. They were caught off-guard and didn't know what to say. Since Hercules had helped them resolve their issue with the waiter, they allowed him to sit with them.

'My name is Hercules. I am a guest in your town. I'm here for a few days for some work,' said Hercules, introducing himself. 'May I know your names?' Hercules extended a hand of friendship.

'Yes, why not? I'm Alok. He is Angad. She is Pooja. And she is Jessica. We come here almost every day. Pooja and I are management students. Angad and Jessica are looking for jobs. We come here to share our joys and sorrows,' Alok introduced everyone.

'It's a pleasure meeting you all. We shall continue meeting and share the secret of happiness beyond joys and sorrows,' said Hercules and went away, leaving them puzzled.

After dinner Hercules took out *The Path to Peace* from his bag with great reverence and started reading it. As he gained more and more from this book, it turned into a holy book for him. His own perspective was broadening and he felt it was his moral responsibility to lead people out of suffering.

Hercules had started going for a morning walk by the sea every day. The rising sun on the horizon never failed to fill him with joy. He felt that the natural rhythm of the rising and setting sun represented the joys and sorrows in human life.

Late in the evening, Hercules came to the Young Hut—the aptly named place where the young people usually gathered. He spotted the group he had met the previous day and approached them.

'Hello! How are you all?' Asked Hercules with enthusiasm. They welcomed him with smiles and invited him to sit with them. They had developed some respect for him after their last encounter.

Angad initiated the conversation. 'Something tells me that you enjoy helping others.'

'Oh yes, I do,' affirmed Hercules and began chatting with them to get to know them better.

'Can I share one of my problems with you?' Angad asked him after a brief lull in the conversation.

'With pleasure.'

'For the past two years I've been trying very hard to get a job, but I haven't been successful. Sometimes I'm told that I'll get a call soon and sometimes another candidate is selected because of his connections. At home, my family cannot understand my problem and they blame me. I'm being victimized by both parties. My elder brother earns a hefty pay. At every step I am compared to him. For any decision that has to be taken at home, my views are always ignored. My brother's friends are welcomed, while my friends are ridiculed. All this makes me feel utterly despondent. I feel that there is no joy left in my life. Can you suggest something that can help me out of this situation?'

'For this you will need to dig deep within yourself and scrutinize your thoughts.'

'How do I do that?'

'You will need to understand some basic truths. One of them is: there is no suffering in this world. Suffering lies in the thoughts that arise in reaction to the world. When we stamp—or believe to be true—our assumptions about the incidents in our life, then our thoughts increase manifold. First of all, you need to stop stamping on the events occurring in your life. Stamping means: fixing your opinion upon an event. In other words, believing that the thoughts which arise in your mind in reaction to an event are the truth. Like you said just now, "I feel that there is no joy left in my life because I haven't got a job." This is stamping.'

'Oh! Is that so? I never thought of it this way.'

'The truth is that you have neither lost anything, nor can you ever lose anything. In fact, whatever is happening to you is exactly what you need today. This is what you need. Understand this important statement. If you can understand this, then you will never feel sad, depressed or angry in your life.'

'You mean to say that not getting a job is my need today?'

'Yes. It is possible that a very good job is waiting for you. Maybe a bigger plan is in store for you. Perhaps the courses that you're doing until you get a job are important for developing your capabilities and for helping you progress faster in your future. Once you start thinking in this manner, you will get many answers telling you that not getting a job is what you need today.'

'I'm not entirely convinced. Can you please explain this concept a bit further?'

'Of course. Let me give you an example. A child is forced by his father to eat bitter gourd every day. An onlooker may think that the child is being tormented. But he doesn't know that the child is suffering from a disease that can be cured by eating bitter gourd. When people see that the child hates eating bitter gourd but is being forced to eat it, they might stamp the incident as a great injustice being meted out to the child. But that is not the truth. Therefore, understand that whatever is happening to someone is his need for the moment. So, Angad, you need to realize that your thought, "I am not getting a job and that's a great injustice", is merely stamping done by you. It's just your belief.'

Everybody was listening with rapt attention and they nodded in approval. They were all impressed by this new line of thought.

Hercules continued, 'You look at an event and immediately stamp on it without having complete knowledge. Then you suffer. When you come to know the reality, you lament, "There was no need for me to suffer so much!" You get this insight after understanding the reality, but what about the so-called suffering that you have already undergone?'

'So-called suffering?' Alok asked.

'Yes, it is just a so-called suffering because it disappears once you realize the truth. So, remember to stop and investigate before stamping upon any situation, event, thought or scene. Do not instantly believe it to be the truth.'

'But what about the fact that my people taunt me and criticize me all the time? Is that a stamping too?' asked Angad.

'Let's look at this in another way,' said Hercules. 'When you make frequent statements that such and such things happen to me, you unconsciously ingrain this thinking deep into your subconscious. The result is that you demand this very thing again from nature. And when this demand is met, you say, "Did you see that? Didn't I tell you this would happen? I always knew that this is exactly what would happen." Thus, in ignorance, you keep placing the same orders with the universe so as to prove yourself right. But now, when you will investigate your thoughts, you will start receiving the best things in life. This inner investigation will stop you from demanding the same old things and proving to yourself and others that injustice has been done to you.'

'You mean to say that "my people taunt me" is a statement I frequently make in order to prove myself right and, in the process, unknowingly ask for this same thing to happen again?' Angad was bewildered.

'Yes, that's how it is. No one does this knowingly, but in ignorance you begin to think against the laws of nature, and nature does not change its laws. If a little child puts its hand in fire, nature doesn't say, "This is a little child. Let me not burn his hand." Whether it is a child or a grown-up, the hand is going to burn if put in fire. Similarly, by thinking negative thoughts you unknowingly work against the laws of nature. The universal law says, "If this person is thinking such and such a thing, it means that this is what he wants. Let his wish be fulfilled." Thus, you unknowingly attract all the wrong things towards yourself.'

'We all feel that, somewhere or the other, injustice is being meted out to us. Now we shall all investigate our injustices. Will you please spend some time with us every day and help us out?' Alok asked politely.

'Yes, why not? We shall look into all your issues one by one.

Tomorrow we shall hear from you, Alok, about the injustice that you think has been meted out to you. Now order your food before it's time for the restaurant to close!'

Alok ordered some food and said, 'Usually we come here after having dinner. Most of the times we survive on tea or coffee.'

Hercules laughed and said, 'Enjoy the feast today.'

They smiled and ate their food, after which they left for their homes.

Hercules went to his room and read the chapter on injustice in *The Path to Peace* so that he could clarify Alok's issues the next day.

In the morning, he went for his usual walk. He was very happy with the changes he was experiencing in himself. He found it miraculous that he always stayed calm and collected nowadays. Also, the right answers occurred to him at the right time. He realized that divine wisdom had started seeping inside him.

In the evening, Hercules approached the Young Hut. The group was sipping coffee and waiting for him. He greeted everyone cheerfully and took a seat. Alok offered him a cup of coffee.

Hercules sipped at it and asked, 'All right, Alok. Tell me, what injustice is being meted out to you?'

Alok began, 'The professors at my college are very partial. They give better grades to their favourite students and, despite my good performance, they give me lower grades. This injustice disturbs me a great deal. What do you have to say about this?'

'First of all, tell me if you guys have tried the technique of investigation that I spoke about yesterday,' Hercules asked.

Angad said, 'I did contemplate upon the injustices happening to me, but could you explain the process of investigation through some examples?'

'Yes, I will give some examples. But first I'd like to hear your thoughts.'

'Sure. I'll tell you what I understood after contemplation. Later, we'd like to know the answer to Alok's problem,' said Angad. 'I asked myself, "Am I absolutely certain that I was the most deserving candidate in that interview? Perhaps somebody else was more capable than me. His selection was apparently an injustice to me, but for him it could have been the justice he was waiting for. Then what is the truth? Was it really injustice to me or was it just my way of looking at the incident? If I didn't get this job, it does not mean that my chances of getting another job are over. Have I fallen a victim to the belief that my chances are slim because of the rising unemployment and the current recession? Is this belief keeping me from landing a job?"'

'You're thinking in the right direction,' Hercules said.

Angad continued, 'If my family treats me callously, does it mean that their motive is bad? They are worried about me, which may be forcing them to behave this way. Or perhaps I'm carrying the guilt of unemployment on my shoulders, which makes me speak rudely to them? Because of my failure to land a job, I've become unusually sensitive to anything negative. All those things that I used to ignore earlier are bothering me now. This contemplation has broadened my perspective a great deal.'

Hercules was pleased with what he heard.

But Alok was getting impatient. 'Please tell me how to investigate my problem,' he implored.

'All right, all of you can understand the art of inner investigation through a story I'm going to narrate,' said Hercules. 'Once upon a time, there was a king. His heart's desire was that all his subjects always receive justice. In order to ensure that, he would roam his kingdom incognito so that he could keep an eye on all that happened in his territory. He came to know that his kingdom was crawling with thieves and thugs. The king managed to nab each one of them and provide relief to his subjects. He also saw a lot of suffering in his empire. There were many poor and homeless people who faced a lot of trouble. He sat with them, discussed their problems and found solutions for them. Thus, he resolved all the difficulties of his people by investigating thoroughly.'

'We can understand what you're hinting at,' smiled Angad.

Hercules elaborated, 'In this analogy, you are the king. You have to roam the kingdom of your mind, every nook and corner, and search for thieves and thugs, i.e. the unpleasant thoughts that rob you of your wealth. You have to investigate these thoughts to their roots, so that the wealth of peace and happiness abounds through all your being. If you love justice the way the king did, you will begin this work at once. You have to search within for all the thoughts of victimization that are lurking in the corners of your mind—the thoughts that make you miserable. You have to investigate and go to their roots. Whenever thoughts of injustice appear in your mind, wait. Don't stamp on them immediately. Look for the false beliefs at the base of these thoughts. Your investigation will disclose the real problem to you.'

'What is justice and injustice? Please throw some light on this so that we can investigate deeply like the king,' they said.

'Okay, listen carefully. In this world, many events occur at the same time. In these events, some people are treated well, some badly. Each individual looks at this treatment as justice or injustice based upon his current level of understanding. In other words, if the treatment he gets is good, he thinks that justice has been done, and if the treatment he gets is bad, he thinks that injustice has been done. These are just fallacies. The fact is that nature is giving us some signals that we need to understand.'

'If I'm getting low grades at college, what is nature telling me?' asked Alok.

'Through this, nature is telling you to work harder and smarter. It is trying to teach you to adjust to the situation. It is offering you a chance to introspect and become more efficient. This event should become your motivation to achieve your ambitions. If you are able to think in this manner, then all the seemingly negative incidents will become stepping stones for you.'

'Wow! It's so important to learn the art of catching signals from nature.'

'You need to learn to look at the injustices being meted out to you from a positive perspective. When people face injustice, they too begin to commit atrocities on themselves. They can see the external injustice but not the internal injustice. Alok, now you have to investigate within and find out the injustices that you are committing against yourself. Find out what positive things you are preventing from coming to you. Find out when you became a piece of brass instead of becoming a magnet.'

'What do you mean by that?'

'Whenever resistance against something builds up inside you or, in other words, when you have constant complaints about something, you become a piece of brass. This prevents many positive things from coming towards you. This is the biggest injustice you can do to yourself. You may have committed it in ignorance, but it is injustice all the same. Therefore, if you want to put a stop to the external injustice, you must first investigate where and how you do injustice to yourself.'

'Yes, I experienced failure in a few interviews and now I go for interviews in a depressed state of mind. Now I understand that I am being unjust to myself by doing that,' said Angad.

'You've got it!' said Hercules. 'Look into all that has happened in your life until now. This exploration will bring many things to light. If you think, 'This is wrong. It shouldn't have happened this way,' then understand that you have not yet learnt to look at injustice in the right manner. The injustice happening to you is giving you a lot of information about yourself. It is telling you that, at some level, you want this injustice. First, a demand is created—only then is it fulfilled. No action is ever one-sided. Whatever happens always happens with the consent of both parties. If there is injustice being done on one end, there is someone ready to receive it on the other.'

'Does that mean I'm demanding the injustice that my people are meting out to me?' Angad was sceptical.

'Let's understand this point. You think that your people always insult you by saying hurtful things. It is this thought process of yours that creates the demand for injustice. Therefore, do not stamp on any event. When you stamp on something, i.e. when you believe it, you bring that thing into your life. It means that your thinking in a particular manner encourages the other person to behave in a particular manner. When you formed this opinion for the first time, you should have investigated into the matter and eliminated those thoughts—then you wouldn't have reached this stage.'

'I shall contemplate on this some more,' said Angad.

'You need to stop this injustice now. Therefore, investigate all the mistakes that you have committed due to which you are bringing negativity into your life. One external event can awaken you forever and stop you from attracting injustice—provided you have that understanding.'

Silence prevailed for a while, before Jessica broke it. 'Can I say something?'

'Sure, without any hesitation,' said Hercules.

'My landlord has taken a year's deposit from me but is asking me to vacate the house even before the year is over. Seeing his unjust behaviour I feel like filing a court case against him,' said Jessica heatedly.

'Sure, go ahead and file a complaint. But do so in the court within! You are being unjust to yourself. Therefore, you must appeal to the inner court.'

Jessica didn't know what to say. She stared at Hercules, trying to understand his words.

Hercules explained, 'If the victim of an injustice is told that he himself is being unjust, he'll say, "What are you talking about? You should guide me—tell me which court to appeal in, suggest a lawyer who has never lost a case. Instead, you're spouting nonsense!" The mind wants such solutions.'

'Then what should I do?'

'You should appeal in a court where money doesn't play a role. And that is the court within. File your case there and contemplate upon it. The discussion that takes place within will throw a new light on things. There you can see clearly that the event has occurred in your life to teach you something. You will understand that your current negative thought process can become a hurdle in your progress. This event has come to help you remove all the obstacles from your path, i.e. it has come to change your thought process. If your thought process is right, then you will be able to overcome all the hurdles in your path. If your thinking is faulty, you will be placing the same old orders with the universe and, consequently, receiving the same old things. The same thoughts will arise in your mind and you will receive proofs for your beliefs as well. You will then say to yourself, "I am right in thinking what I think. I stand vindicated. "I have so much proof now that even if god comes to earth and tells me otherwise, I shall not agree."'

'You mean to say that I should not take any step against my landlord?' asked Jessica cynically.

'No, I'm not telling you not to take any action. You need to take the appropriate steps, as per the law, to solve the problem. The law will take its own course. But you must learn how to think when problems appear in your life—this is extremely important.'

They all were listening, rapt. When Hercules stopped, they said, 'Tomorrow we'll come prepared with our investigations using the method you have taught us.'

The next day, Hercules returned from his morning walk, he came across Bhaiji. Bhaiji had been keeping an eye on Hercules. 'I see you visiting the Young Hut quite often these days. What's the matter?' he asked.

'Yes, a group of youngsters comes there every evening. They want me to help them with some of their problems. I too enjoy helping them out. So, after finishing my maintenance work, I join them and make them investigate their problems,' replied Hercules.

'In that case, we should change the name of that hut to Introspection

Hut. What do you say? People will come and ask you questions. Your job will be to satisfy them,' said Bhaiji.

'That will be wonderful!' Hercules was thrilled.

In the evening, Hercules got busy decorating the Introspection Hut. When the group joined him some time later, they were surprised to see the changes. Hercules explained the reason for these changes and said, 'My advice is now available to everyone.' Hercules looked at Alok's and Jessica's faces and added, 'Today you both look happy. I think it's the result of your internal exploration.'

'You're right, sir. Yesterday we investigated our thoughts in writing and we want to read out the findings to you,' they said.

'Sure, please begin.'

They took their favourite places and Alok started reading.

'My college professors are very partial. They give better grades to their favourite students and are unjust to me. When I contemplated upon this complaint, I understood the following points:

- It is my stamping that the professors are partial.
- If I remove my stamping and beliefs, then the problem looks very small.
- Even though I think that my performance is good, perhaps the others have been performing better.
- If this event makes me develop a spirit of healthy competition, it is a boon for me.
- If this event makes me work in an organized manner, it will prove to be a stepping stone for me.
- If all my points of contemplation are positive, then how can

this event be unjust? Why am I feeling miserable and doing injustice to myself? When I stop being unjust to myself, others too will stop being unjust to me.'

Hercules was very happy with Alok's investigation. These insights helped the others as well.

Jessica eagerly asked, 'Can I read now?'

'Yes, sure,' said Hercules.

'The landlord is being unjust to me. He has taken the deposit for a year but is asking me to vacate earlier. I contemplated upon this grudge thus:

- I have attracted this event in my life because of my belief that landlords always trouble tenants.

- The very fact that the landlord is being unjust to me means that, at some level, I wanted injustice done to me, albeit unknowingly. This was the order I had placed with the universe.

- This event occurred in my life based upon the law of demand and supply. Therefore, I am responsible for it.

- Nature is sending me a signal to start wanting and expecting justice and not injustice—only then can something new enter my life.

- As long as I am engaged in proving my belief right, all this will continue to happen.

- I am doing great injustice to myself in other spheres of life too. I keep avoiding the gym, I eat fried food and junk food, I stay up till late at night and don't let my body get enough sleep. Thus, I am being unjust to my body. By thinking negative thoughts, I am being unjust to my mind too.

'After this exploration, my mind has taken an inward turn and I feel connected to my inner self,' chirped Jessica.

Hercules praised them saying, 'Both of you have investigated in the right manner and you have already gotten the results! In a similar way, you need to bring each thought of suffering and victimization to light and uproot it.'

Angad and Pooja were also inspired by what they had been hearing.

Angad said, 'I want to tell you something.'

'Please go ahead,' said Hercules.

'As I told you earlier, I've been looking for a job for the past two years. People don't respect me because I am unemployed. Wherever I go, whether it is a wedding or some other social function, people look down upon me. Once someone sent a proposal for my marriage but then turned me down because of my unemployed status. "Who will give their daughter to him?", people said and hurt my emotions. Isn't this gross injustice?'

'Today, I have brought my teacher with me so that you all can receive justice. Let us all take guidance from him on this subject,' said Hercules.

They all were baffled. Hercules carefully took out *The Path to Peace* from his bag and kept it on the table. He opened it reverently and started reading.

> Until now, man has been evaluating events on the basis of justice or injustice. Actually, he should first understand the true meaning of justice and injustice.
>
> When someone doesn't treat you well or is unjust to you, ask yourself, 'Did the event upset me or did the thoughts that followed upset me?' The reality will then become clear. You

will learn that you became upset because of the thoughts that followed the event. If the thought, 'Injustice has been done to me,' had not occurred to you, you wouldn't have been upset. No one gave this thought to you. No one gave this instruction in writing. You yourself brought in this thought and became unhappy.

'This means that the thought "I am a victim of injustice" is responsible for my suffering?' asked Angad.

'That's right,' said Hercules and continued reading.

> No event ever brings suffering with it. Suffering has not been created in this world. But man has been given so much freedom that he is allowed to suffer if he so chooses. No animal suffers unhappiness because animals do not have choice. Man has choice. He can decide whether he wants to live in joy or in sorrow. Man creates joy and sorrow through his thoughts.

'This sounds very illogical,' murmured Alok.

'It may sound illogical, but it is the truth. No event ever produces suffering—all suffering is produced by our thoughts following that event. Let us understand this more clearly through an example,' said Hercules and resumed reading from the book.

> A man's uncle lived in America while the man lived in India. One day his uncle suddenly passed away, but the man was not sad because he was not aware of it. If he had heard the news of his uncle's demise, he would have had sad thoughts. But before he could receive the news, he himself died. His uncle's death caused him no suffering in his lifetime.
>
> Now think: what is the actual cause of sorrow? Is it the event—in this case, the death? Or is it the thoughts that would have followed the news of the death? This example should make it

clear that it is not the event that causes suffering. The main culprit is the thoughts that follow.

'You mean the thought, "The girl's parents rejected me", is the cause of my sorrow?' Angad asked.

'That's right,' replied Hercules and continued reading.

> If someone rejects you and, as a result, you gain courage and tenacity, wouldn't that injustice have turned into justice for you? If you decouple your thoughts from the injustice and keep your focus on the benefits accruing from it, your thoughts will find a new direction. Then you will be able to declare that you are no longer a victim. All you have to do is provide the right direction to your thoughts. Everything else will take care of itself.

'This event taught me how not to commit injustice against myself, but I'm still unhappy that my parents took the girl's side and not mine,' said Angad.

'The book explains this too. Listen,' said Hercules.

> Many a time, if your elders agree with you, you feel as though justice has been done. But the reality is that you are still deprived of justice. The justice imparted by your elders makes you happy for a while, but justice that satisfies the mind can make only half the people happy. The rest still remain unhappy. True justice is that which makes everyone happy. This is the justice of the inner court. How do you keep the scales of justice in balance? How do you maintain inner peace and purity? You have to learn this. On one side, there are the tendencies and habits of your body and mind; on the other, your body and mind waver in some situations. You need to strike the right balance.

> By attaining these insights, not only are you gaining justice,

you are also becoming a white-coat lawyer. Henceforth, you will bestow justice yourself and not depend upon others for it. Whenever you see injustice in the world, you will first do justice to yourself. Otherwise, you will keep getting carried away by wrong thoughts and become unjust to yourself.

Say a person is walking down the street and some unruly people hit him and run away. Now, if you slap yourself after looking at this perceived injustice, will that be just? That is not just but that is exactly what you do. You see something and start punishing yourself by thinking negative thoughts. You are unaware of this because it is happening in the background and is invisible. Nobody has pointed this out to you before. You have always seen others do it, so you do it too. When people meet each other, all they talk about is, 'This is what happened today. I saw such and such an incident. I heard about such and such a thing. Today, the world is going to the dogs.' In this way, each one is stamping on his thoughts. If this carries on, how can justice be served? Henceforth, whenever thoughts like these appear in your mind, you must exhibit inner strength and say, 'I will not stamp upon this thought. I will not believe in it and allow myself to become unhappy.'

'I think I am beginning to understand this,' said Angad thoughtfully.

Pooja, who had been listening quietly all this time said, 'One question has been bothering me for a long time. I haven't got my answer even after investigating within. I feel that god has done great injustice to me by taking my mother away from me.' Pooja had lost her mother some years ago after a protracted illness. She missed her mother sorely.

'Let me read out a part that addresses this issue,' said Hercules in a sympathetic tone.

Every creature in this universe is being looked after, but only man thinks that if he has lost someone dear it means that he is not being looked after. In reality, everyone is being looked after with great care, whether it is a tiny ant or a little creature living at the bottom of the sea. Man makes his own definitions. He thinks that 'being looked after' means such and such a thing. If the events in his life do not fit this definition, he thinks he is not being looked after. In the same way, due to lack of knowledge of life after death, he bemoans a death saying, 'This is terrible.' His thinking is narrow. Hence, he wants his near and dear ones to live with him all his life so that he does not have to suffer the pain of their absence. Even if it means that they will have to suffer the pains of hell while living their life, he wants them to live for his happiness.

If your love is true, you will allow the person who wants to die to die—because this is justice for him. You can do true justice only when you acquire complete knowledge of this life and of life after death. You cannot do true justice with half-baked knowledge. What you were regarding as injustice until now was, in fact, not injustice at all. Hence, do not stamp on it as injustice. Just see it as it is, and investigate it.

Pooja felt lighter after listening to this. So far, she had been looking at her mother's death from her own perspective. It had never occurred to her that there could be another dimension to the event. She had decided that her mother's death was an act of injustice committed by god. Now she realized that by not accepting her mother's death, she was doing injustice to her mother.

'All right, now we shall not let any injustice happen to our stomachs,' Angad joked. He called the waiter and ordered some food. After attaining a new understanding, everyone enjoyed their food and headed back home.

The next morning, Hercules did not follow the usual path for his walk.

After walking for half an hour, he saw some ships anchored at a jetty. He knew that there was a port for merchant ships at some distance from the resort. His curiosity took him closer. As he approached it, he noticed Bhaiji. 'How come you're here?' he asked.

A startled Bhaiji replied, 'I import some stuff by sea for my business. I've come to check on that.' Then, quickly changing the topic he said, 'How is your Introspection Hut doing? Yesterday I was passing by and I noticed that you are quite an expert at getting your point across.'

Hercules smiled and thought to himself, 'He doesn't know that all this has been possible thanks to the blessings of the Goddess.' He took his leave—his homework was pending.

Bhaiji was worried. Hercules had been at the resort for several days but the consignment for the priest had still not arrived.

Hercules had started to go and sit in the Introspection Hut from 7 p.m. onwards. He had taken full responsibility of cleaning and decorating that hut. Alok and his group were regular visitors, but some other people too had started visiting, attracted by the name. Sometimes they used to listen to Hercules speak, while at other times they discussed among themselves to solve their problems.

This evening there were a lot of people in the hut. They had been listening to Hercules' wise suggestions for the past few days. Hercules looked at them and asked, 'Do any of you want to ask me something?'

A lady started sobbing. After a while, she got a grip on herself and said, 'The kind of pain that I have suffered at the hands of my cruel mother-in-law is something that should not happen to anybody. About ten years ago, she falsely accused me of theft in front of so many guests. Later, everyone came to know the truth. But I still can't forget the humiliation.'

Hercules said to the lady, 'You have been coming here for the past few days. You must have heard me talking about investigation, beliefs, stamping, labelling, etc.'

'Yes, I have heard these words and I have also seen people finding solutions to their problems here. That is why I mustered the courage to speak to you.'

'That's good. We shall address your issue right now. The first thing you can do is to ask yourself, "If I am suffering from an injustice done by my in-laws ten years ago, then who has inflicted more suffering upon me—my in-laws or myself?" That unpleasant event did take place, but for how much time did those people trouble you? Ten hours? Ten days? Ten months? But you have been tormenting yourself for the past ten years by recalling that event over and over again! What about that? Who is the bigger culprit? It's true that your mother-in-law made you suffer, but do you realize how much suffering you are inflicting upon yourself by repeatedly replaying that event in your mind? Who's the one actually making us suffer? The investigation into this question is the beginning of the end of suffering.'

The lady was astonished. Hercules carried on, 'In this way, when someone investigates into his misery—with understanding and in the right direction—he doesn't remain unhappy. He feels happy. Therefore, first stop inflicting suffering upon yourself. Then you can expect others to stop inflicting suffering upon you. Before inner investigation, you cannot see that you're causing pain to yourself through your thoughts. Once you understand, you'll say, 'Oh my god! I never thought about this. I'm such a fool. I've been causing myself pain by remembering that event again and again."

'I have been making the same mistake,' the lady agreed.

'When you start thinking in this manner and investigate within yourself, you will not only stop complaining about others but also stop torturing yourself. At the same time, you will understand that you have to look for the complaint and its solution not in others, but within yourself.

'Perform your investigation standing in front of a mirror. Ask yourself, "Why are you causing sorrow to yourself?" Earlier, you used to blame others saying, "Why has this person inflicted pain upon me?" But now you will question yourself. This experiment will help you discover your own nature as well as the truth. It is important to discover the answer to "Am I doing the same thing that I'm complaining about in others?"

'Suppose someone throws abuses at you and you feel bad. In reply, you too hurl abuses at him and say, 'Don't ever abuse anyone again!' You do not realize that you are also swearing at him. This is similar to what your reaction might be if somebody writes something on the outer walls of your house. You might get furious and write on the walls yourself: "No one should write anything here without my permission." Thus, you don't realize that you're doing exactly what you are complaining about.'

The lady was dumbfounded.

Hercules said, 'Let us all close our eyes and ponder over the question: if someone had slapped you ten years ago and you keep slapping yourself every day by recollecting that event, then who is the bigger offender? Who is more cruel? Who should you complain against?

Who should you file an FIR against in the police station of your mind? Dive deep within and search: what complaints have you been harbouring in your life? Against whom?'

Everyone deliberated upon this point and accepted that we give ourselves more pain than the people we blame.

After that, another lady began narrating her problem. She said, 'Wherever I go, I get saddled with work—at home, in the office. And if I think of taking a break and going to my parents' home, I have to work there too! I often wonder why this injustice is being meted out to me.'

Hercules explained, 'If you need to work everywhere, it means that you are being given an opportunity to work. Whenever you get an opportunity, you should happily take full advantage of it. A porter lifts huge weights and so does a weightlifter. The porter calls it a burden while the weightlifter calls it an opportunity to improve his health. Now you have to decide whether to work like a porter or a weightlifter. You are getting an opportunity to work. So work happily and freely. Even if you are saddled with lots of work, you can only carry out one task at a time. Although the second hand in a clock needs to keep ticking forever, it has to tick only once in one second. Likewise, you too have to do just one thing at a time. The thought of doing a whole lot of work together is what makes work seem like a burden.'

This point seemed to resonate with the lady. She said, 'From now on, I'll start working with the spirit of a weightlifter.'

At 8 p.m., Alok and his group came in. The atmosphere seemed to be joyful. Thanks to their investigations, it had become easy for them to remain happy even under adverse circumstances.

Sensing that Jessica wanted to say something, Hercules asked her,

'Do you wish to talk?'

Several issues were troubling her. She began speaking with great passion, 'I've seen that people often have to pay hefty sums to gain admission to educational institutes. It has become next to impossible for the common man to educate their children. Similarly, corruption has spread far and wide in hospitals, government offices and other departments. Good conduct and honesty have lost their meaning. Our entire system is corrupt. Someone should definitely raise a voice against this. Otherwise, how will an average person run his household? I want to do something that will bring justice to the people.'

Hercules said, 'It's good that you think that you should help to get rid of this or that injustice. But first you must stop the injustice that is happening to your own self. If you can't stop this injustice, then how will you stop the injustices happening to others? Only a free person can help others become free.'

Hercules opened his magic book, bowed in reverence and said, 'I shall read out the answer to your problem.'

> When people say that they want to stop injustice in society, they need to be gently reminded that they have to free themselves first. If you want to free others and liberate them from suffering, you will have to start with yourself. You need to stop committing injustice against yourself. If you can't stop doing injustice to yourself, how can you stop the injustice happening to others? How will you get the strength to do so? Therefore, you must first build your strength. When you have done that, you will only feel gratitude for the unjust behaviour of others because they made you stop committing injustice against yourself. Now you will look at everything with new eyes. Then your very presence will stop injustice.

An individual who is not free is a slave. A slave unknowingly brings about only slavery wherever he goes. It is but natural that people do to others what they do to themselves. The one who cannot forgive himself can never forgive others. His body language will always tell others that they are no good. Thus, injustice will always remain present somewhere. People read sensational news in the newspapers or watch it on television. They think, "Oh my god! What is happening to this world?" If you want to help free the world, you have to free yourself first. If you don't find your freedom, people will continue doing injustice to you. If you can free yourself, there is the possibility of helping others become free. When you cannot liberate just one person—your own self—how can you help liberate millions? Therefore, begin with yourself. Free yourself first.

'This is an amazing truth! Something that we've never thought about before! Now we know where to start if we want to actually help free others. We must first stop the injustice we do to ourselves and build our inner strength,' said a thrilled Jessica. 'And in order to stop the injustice we do to ourselves, we need to investigate the unhappy thoughts that are circulating in our minds. We need to cleanse our minds of those thoughts. For that, we should converse with our thoughts. We should give them an opportunity to speak.'

Hercules added, 'Yes, when you tell your thoughts to talk about the injustice they themselves have been committing against you, they will feel embarrassed. Counterfeit currency can only be used until someone doubts its authenticity. When you start doubting your thoughts, they will quieten down. This is the only way to achieve freedom.'

'Great. Let us read further,' Jessica said eagerly.

If you are able to liberate yourself, then the coloured glasses through which you have been looking at life will vanish. Once that happens, new things will be revealed to you. You may not understand all the new things immediately but, with whatever you have understood, start investigating how and where you are committing injustices against yourself.

Gradually, you will come to know that we have come to earth to understand all of this. The earth is an arrangement by itself. Understanding justice and injustice is a part of this arrangement. There are some people in this world who fight against injustice all their lives but stay unhappy themselves. You are not being asked to ignore injustice. You must fight against it—but do so in the right manner. If you are thinking of fighting for justice, you should do it with the right mind-set. Most people do it in a state of unhappiness. Whatever you do to yourself, you will do the same to others. In other words, you will make them achieve freedom in one aspect while pushing them into slavery in another.

In order to do true justice, you will need to explore your thoughts and get stabilized in your inner experience of being. Then you will thank god for this guidance. Earlier, you were pulling the thread from the wrong end and hoping that it would undo the knot, but it kept getting more and more entangled. There is injustice from outside as well as inside. When you yourself are not completely clear, how will you advise others? First, enlighten yourself completely. Prepare yourself so well that not even a single corner inside you remains in darkness. As you gain more wisdom, as your understanding deepens, you will say that now this injustice is not needed. When you stop doing injustice to yourself, you will start being just to others. When you see injustice happening to others, you will want them to arrive at the right understanding. This is because you have realized that they are going through this injustice for no reason. At that time, a question will arise in your mind: Why is man suffering from something which hasn't even been created? When an item is not on the menu, when it has not been cooked in the kitchen, why is man eating it?

Hercules stopped reading. There was pin-drop silence. Everyone felt a new understanding germinating within.

Hercules said, 'I have a message for you all. Please investigate your perceived injustices so deeply that the injustices done by you against yourself stop totally. Just think: if one act of injustice stops all injustice from entering your life, can it still be called injustice? Won't it be the ultimate act of justice?'

Enthralled by his wisdom, everyone thanked Hercules profusely before leaving. It was 10 p.m. Hercules went to his room.

The next morning, as Hercules left for his walk, yesterday's discussion was still on his mind. Yesterday, he had become quite solemn. While speaking about justice and injustice he had received a new insight. Until now, he too had been looking at the injustice done against him from a different angle. Whenever he had a fight with Radha, he used to think, 'Her entry into my life is god's injustice. My aunt had brought this marriage proposal. She knew Radha's nature very well. Why did she choose her for me? Hasn't she committed an injustice against me by doing so?' This thought would prick Hercules like a thorn. But after last night's contemplation he realized that, thanks to Radha's nature, he had come to know his inner self. Thanks to Radha's behaviour, he came face to face with his ego. In reality, Radha had not committed an injustice, but the greatest justice. He realized, 'Radha and I are opposites who complement each other.'

However, melancholy set in as he remembered his children. It had been ages since he had last seen them. He thought, 'Why has nature been unjust to me by separating me from my children?' He then remembered how he told everyone to investigate within, in the Introspection Hut. Now, it was his turn to apply those teachings.

He investigated within and came up with some points:

- Perhaps nature wishes to impart some special training to me.
- It is possible that what seems like injustice today may actually turn out to be a blessing in disguise tomorrow.
- When I go back after liberating myself completely and after becoming strong in the real sense of the word, I will be able to give the right values to my children. In addition, I will also prove to be a good husband.
- Then, perhaps, this is the ultimate justice for me.

Guidance from *The Path to Peace* had eliminated his wrong beliefs. He resolved to return home pure and pious by becoming free from all his made-up stories. After the walk, he returned to the resort.

Bhaiji was having tea when he saw Hercules approaching. Hercules had sown seeds of love and harmony amongst the hotel staff as well. They were all deeply impressed by him. Happiness had increased their efficiency at work. Bhaiji was aware of this change. He too had begun thinking well of Hercules. Now his conscience would not let him send the shipment—which, for some reason, still hadn't arrived—to the priest, while keeping this honest man in the dark. He thought, 'He knows me as a devotee of the Goddess. What if he comes to know my reality? And even if he doesn't, how can I deceive a true devotee? Won't that be a sin?' His train of thought was disturbed when his mobile phone rang. The call was from the police station. They had detained his son and were asking Bhaiji to come as soon as possible.

For a while Bhaiji didn't know what had hit him. He was anxious to know what his son had done to warrant this. He rushed to the police station. The police had detained five youngsters who were found high on drugs in a remote corner of the beach. One of them was his son. Bhaiji used his influence and managed to bring him home. He did not have the slightest inkling that his son had become a drug addict. He was dumbstruck. He could see his own hand in it. He realized that while he had been sowing seeds of poison for others, this poisonous vine had crept into his own home.

Hercules was with him during all this. He tried his best to comfort Bhaiji and took full responsibility for curing his son's addiction. He first got the boy admitted to a rehabilitation centre where he was told that the boy needed only a short stay as he was a recent addict. Both Hercules and Bhaiji were relieved to hear this. Hercules visited the boy regularly and supported him during this difficult period. With patience and persistence, he started developing a friendship with the boy. The boy slowly began to discuss his issues with Hercules, who began teaching him about inner investigation.

He would counsel him and also read from the magic book to help him resolve his conflicts. Soon, the boy was discharged and brought home. He had progressed steadily and Bhaiji was happy to see him normal again.

During this time, the shipment that Bhaiji had been eagerly waiting for came in. However, the recent events had made him start repenting. He now wanted to become a true devotee of the Goddess. He took an oath to reform himself, and called for Hercules. He earnestly thanked Hercules for his stay and handed him a letter for the priest. He also gave a hefty sum for the temple and saw him off with respect.

Hercules sat in the bus and started analysing the days he had spent at the resort. Before coming here, he had been instrumental in transforming the lives of Jitendra and Jagruti. He realized that he had now been successful in changing the thought process of four others: Alok, Angad, Pooja and Jessica. Bhaiji's son too had improved, but Hercules did not feel as if his entire thinking had changed. He needed some more support and maturity to turn his life around. Hercules had handed over the responsibility of the Introspection Hut to Angad before leaving. He had also given him a copy of *The Path to Peace*. He was very happy that he had been able to transform six lives in six months, as instructed by the Goddess. Half his journey was over. Now he was waiting for the priest's next order.

It was Tuesday—the day of the Goddess. A great number of devotees had come to visit the temple. After the prayer, they all queued up for the prasaad. Hercules quietly came and stood at the back of the queue. When his turn came, he extended his hand.

'Hercules! When did you return? You didn't even tell me...' The priest was startled. 'How come he's back before I've received my supply? What's the matter?' He wondered.

Hercules greeted him and handed over Bhaiji's letter and cheque to him saying, 'Bhaiji asked me to give this letter to you. The cheque is a donation for the temple.'

The priest was mystified. He took the letter and the check warily, and told Hercules to rest. Meanwhile, he hurried off to his quarters and started reading the letter.

Dear friend,

Greetings! We have always been good friends and our business partnership has only deepened this bond. According to our plan, I was going to keep Hercules with me until you received your delivery. But life has played such a game with me that now my eyes are open. Man has to pay a price for all his actions. Whatever has happened until now cannot be undone, but in the future I will not be your partner in this heinous crime. I do not wish to add to my sins by cheating a true and honest man like Hercules. I can no longer do this business and let the youth of our country go astray, because our children are also a part of this generation. My decision is final. I advise you to give a serious thought to this as well. I hope that this will not undermine our friendship.

Your well-wisher,

Bhaiji

The priest finished reading the letter and slumped to the floor in disbelief.

FIVE
The Fourth Task of Hercules: Obtaining the Apple —Investigating Illness

For the past two days the priest's head had been spinning with thoughts. He was furious with Hercules but maintained a stoic silence. Hercules had no idea what was happening. The priest's mind was inundated with thoughts like, 'Hercules' penance has ruined my well-established business. His repentance may earn him heavenly rewards, but what about my livelihood? I have to get my daughter married. Where will the money come from? Perhaps my stars are unlucky. Only when Hercules' penance is over, will my luck shine once again.' He couldn't stand Hercules' presence any more. He had forgotten the good that Hercules had done for his sister. He was busy plotting how to get rid of him. Immersed in these thoughts, he fell into a fitful sleep.

At midnight, Hercules woke up from his sleep in pain. He was having terrible cramps in his stomach. He took a painkiller, but to no avail. He kept tossing and turning in bed. The abdominal cramps would not abate. After some time, he was nauseated and had loose motions. His mouth tasted bitter. He felt weak and couldn't get up from the bed. He spent the night in agony.

In the morning, the priest noticed that Hercules was not around, so he went to his room to inquire. He took one look at Hercules' pale face and dry lips and understood the seriousness of the situation. He decided Hercules needed immediate medical attention and took him to a hospital in the neighbouring city. On the way to the hospital, he hatched a plan. 'I'll get Hercules admitted to the hospital and send all his belongings there along with a message that I am going to my sister's house. After he gets well, he can do whatever he wants to do with his life. I'll have nothing to do with him any more.'

The doctor examined Hercules and advised admission. The priest agreed happily. Things were going according to plan. Hercules was given a bed in the general ward. The doctor diagnosed food poisoning. The priest was least concerned. He promised to return in the evening and left.

Hercules' migraine too returned with a vengeance. He couldn't decide which was worse: the stomach-ache or the headache. He felt completely drained, mentally and physically. He called for the doctor and told him about his migraine. The doctor carried out some tests and started his treatment.

Hercules looked around the ward and saw many patients lying in the beds around him. His thoughts went back to his ailment. 'Why does this migraine keep coming back? What did I eat yesterday to get food poisoning? Why have I become so weak?' He kept thinking until he fell asleep.

At noon, the nurse woke him up for lunch. He was not hungry, but the nurse insisted that he have some porridge. The medicines were making him drowsy. He slept until evening and felt slightly better. He got up and took his medicine. He was tired of the hospital in just one day. He felt irritated and distressed. Lying on the bed seemed like some rigorous punishment. Just then, he heard a voice from within, 'Hercules, do not lose this golden opportunity.' These words made him sit up. He realized that he would not find a better opportunity for conducting an investigation within himself.

He felt better and lay down without any more resistance. He closed his eyes. He felt the presence of the Goddess strongly and started speaking to her.

Hercules: Am I placing a repeat order by letting my thoughts revolve around my illness?

Goddess: That's right.

Hercules: If nature is sending me a message through this event, then what is that message?

Goddess: That you need to be more careful about your diet and your health.

Hercules: Why does this migraine keep coming back?

Goddess: Do not take your illness personally. This problem has been given to you so that you investigate it, liberate yourself from it and then help others in liberating themselves from all the negative thoughts that occur when they are ill.

Hercules: Which means that unless I learn this, I will keep suffering?

Goddess: When you will give your thoughts the right direction, you will stop thinking, 'Why has this ailment appeared? Now what will happen to me? How much will I need to spend on my treatment?' Of course, you do need to use your common sense and get proper treatment, but you will be free from feelings of fear, depression and insecurity because you will see the health that is hidden behind the illness.

Hercules: I am feeling better just listening to you. My suffering seems to be reducing. Actually, it is just a matter of changing focus. Now I have understood that we do not carry out the contemplation that illness requires us to do. Instead, we indulge in useless thoughts of suffering.

Goddess: When your thoughts move in the right direction, you become healthy.

Hercules: Mother, this conversation has been very soothing for me. It has given me a new direction for investigation and reflection. Please continue to guide me in this way.

Goddess: I am your inner voice and I am always there for you.

He then drifted off into a restful sleep.

Late in the evening, the doctor examined Hercules. He seemed better than before. The doctor advised him to pay due attention to his diet and take his medicines on time.

Hercules sent a message to the priest to bring his book, *The Path to Peace,* along with him. After some time, the priest arrived at the hospital with not just the book but all of Hercules' belongings. Hercules looked at the priest quizzically.

The priest said, 'I'm leaving for my sister's place. You can go back home once you recover. There's no place for you in the temple any more.'

Hercules was stunned. He wanted to ask what it was that had warranted such a drastic action and how his penance would be completed if the priest deserted him, but the priest had already left. The priest's words and sudden departure disheartened Hercules. He was ill and had also lost his refuge. He didn't know what to do. He felt completely helpless. He had no option but to call out to the Goddess. He surrendered the entire situation to her saying, 'My penance is in your hands now,' and closed his eyes.

In the morning Hercules got up, opened the book and started reading the chapter on health.

Staying happy is the best way to attain total health, even though it may seem difficult at first. For this, you will need to stay away from illusory truths. Illusory truths are the ones that make you unhappy because you take them to be real. These illusory truths take hold of your mind. You need to look beyond these illusions and focus only on the truth.

Hercules closed his eyes. He felt that the priest's abandonment of him was only an illusory truth and in spite of that, his penance would be completed because it was the only truth. He started reading again.

Illusory truths mean those things that look real but are not. When you see it raining heavily, you take it to be the truth. Then you start visualizing all the problems that follow heavy rains. At that time, you do not see the sun that is emerging just beyond the clouds. If you were able to see the sun, the words that would pop out from your mouth would be, 'Thank you God, for the sun!' Therefore, whenever you see heavy rains don't say, 'Oh, it's raining so hard! How troublesome!' Instead, say, 'Thank you God, for the sun!' Similarly, when you look at illness don't say it is causing so much suffering. Rather, look at the health hidden behind the illness and say, 'Thank you God, for health!'

In life, you attract what you see. Hence the need to be vigilant about where your attention is while looking at this world. So, what is it that you are seeing? Diseases are spreading all around. Accidents can occur any time. What if this happens to me… and so on and so forth? If this is what you're seeing, just think how dangerous you are making your life for yourself. You are a piece of iron that has the potential to become a magnet if the truth is imparted to you. But if you remain stuck in illusory truths, you are like brass. You will remain unconscious. When you are convinced about this fact, you will not get entangled in illusory truths.

You don't know how much joy you are losing out on by getting stuck in illusory truths. The fact is that you are harming yourself by getting stuck in them. Sick people only keep thinking of their diseases. In such situations, what will they attract? Nothing but more diseases. Whenever you see the symptoms of any disease, tell yourself, 'I refuse to see the illness. I will see only the health hidden behind it.' Of course, you must also use your common sense and take the medicines prescribed by the doctor.

When you focus only on health and not on disease, you will start seeing the positive results in your life. Medicine, prayer, positive thoughts and inner strength will create miracles and awaken health within you. The moment you start looking at the disease as an illusory truth, the disease begins to disappear. Disease is an illusory truth. Health is the only truth. It is a divine attribute. Indeed, health is waiting to come to you. It is standing at your door thinking, 'When is he going to let go of his illusory truths so that I can enter? This man is holding on to his illness. Why isn't he letting it go?'

Man does not recognize his own power, therefore, he looks at illness. But now when you look at illness, tell yourself, 'This is an illusory truth. I see only health.' This thought will fill you with divine energy. As soon as you start ignoring illusory truths, you will start turning into a magnet and attract positive things towards you. Love, courage, happiness, fulfilment and health will enter your life.

Reading this gave a new direction to Hercules' thoughts. He felt refreshed. He got over his dejection and debilitation to a large extent. After some time, the doctor came in and examined him. He was declared fit to leave in the evening.

As the sun began to set, Hercules got worried. 'Where will I go? The priest must have left by now. The temple gates must be locked. Where can I go? What can I do?' Reluctantly, he packed his bags and got ready to leave. Suddenly, he saw a man on a stretcher being rushed to the operation theatre. He went closer. The man was none other than the priest. Hercules couldn't believe his eyes.

What happened? How did he get hurt? Questions exploded in Hercules' brain. The priest was screaming in pain. Hercules forgot all about his weakness and ran behind the stretcher. He stayed with the priest through all the hospital formalities, medical tests, X-rays, treatments, etc. just like a family member.

In the morning when the priest awoke, he found himself in the hospital. He realized what had happened. The scene of the accident appeared before his eyes like a movie: sitting in the rickshaw to go to the bus stop… a child suddenly running across… the driver trying to dodge him and in the process hitting a pole… the rickshaw overturning… his left leg getting stuck under the rickshaw's rear… some people rescuing him and bringing him here.

The priest saw Hercules sitting beside his bed. He felt a heaviness in his left leg. Hercules looked at him with compassion and gently told him about his fracture. The priest's eyes filled up with tears—he fell a mixture of pain and gratitude for Hercules. He thought, 'If Hercules had not been here, what would have happened to me? I have been so rude to him. I kept measuring the worth of his pure heart on the scale of profit and loss. What a sin I have committed! This man has just recovered from his illness, yet he is standing earnestly at my service. He has been obeying all my orders with great diligence, but how stone-hearted I have been!' These thoughts distressed him and brought tears to his eyes. He sought forgiveness from Hercules.

Hercules asked the priest to calm down. The priest controlled himself and then inquired about the seriousness of his injuries. Hercules informed him, 'Once the swelling reduces, your leg will be put into a cast. There are some abrasions in some places. You need to remain under medical supervision for some days. Please don't worry. I'm with you. This is a simple fracture and it will heal soon.'

'As God wills,' said the priest, turning his face away helplessly and closing his eyes. Hercules let him sleep. He went to the doctor and inquired about the further course of treatment. There he found out that the rickshaw driver had also sustained minor injuries and had been discharged after his wounds had been dressed.

For the past two days, Hercules had been watching a boy of around six or seven years suffering from high fever, next to the priest's bed. His parents Abhay and Anuya were there, looking after him. Sometimes they would argue and blame each other for the child's illness. Hercules had been observing this conflict. Since the priest was resting, he casually started conversing with Abhay and asked him about his son's illness. Hercules' compassionate words made Abhay open up. He began, 'I have only one pain in my life: my son Cheeku keeps falling ill. Sometimes it is viral fever, sometimes malaria, sometimes common cold! His illness fills our hearts with gloom. My wife and I take such good care of him, but still…'

Hercules gave the couple a copy of *The Path to Peace* and asked them to read the chapter 'Causes of Suffering: Beliefs and Stamping'. Since Abhay used to stay back at the hospital at night, he finished reading the chapter very soon. He found the teachings very useful. Before going to bed, he asked Hercules to discuss the topic with him. They went and sat in the hospital corridor to avoid disturbing others.

Abhay said, 'After reading this chapter I have understood how stampings and beliefs become the cause of our suffering. But I am unable to perform an inner investigation of Cheeku's illness. I am unable to come out of my unhappy mental state. Will you offer me some guidance?'

'You may have read in the book that your beliefs and stampings are the cause of your suffering. Therefore investigate whether it is your belief that Cheeku should not fall sick. Do you believe that it is bad to fall sick?' Asked Hercules.

'Yes, that is what I think,' Abhay mumbled.

'Then let us go and ask a doctor if it is wrong for a child to fall sick. The doctor will tell you that children falling sick, falling down during play, being made fun of in school, being given loads of homework and many other things are all a part of growing up. This is a natural process and this process helps in their development.

'If parents protect their children to such an extent that they are not even allowed to fall down, fall sick, or endure any difficulty, how will these children learn? If any problem comes their way, they will wilt. If you don't teach them to face the wind, how will they face a storm? When a plant endures winds, its roots become strong—that is why, on becoming a tree, it can withstand even a storm.

'If you truly love your child, you will allow him to fall sick. Otherwise your fear will enhance the fear of illness inside your child. He will always fear that he is going to fall sick. He will become a hypochondriac. You do not want your child to fall sick but, indirectly, you are contributing to his illness.'

'Oh my god! We are contributing to our son's illness! We would never want that,' exclaimed Abhay.

'Hence the need to let go of the stamping: "It is bad for a child to fall sick," said Hercules. 'Something or the other is happening to the body all the time. Sometimes it is well, sometimes not. When the weather or environment changes, the body gives you feedback. This feedback is a call for action. The body signals you to change your eating habits, start exercising, or do something new since the weather has changed. If the body didn't give you these signals, you would never wake up. Through this feedback, nature is helping you. It is also letting the parents know that the child's routine needs a change.'

'Perhaps you're right. When I look at Cheeku's illness, I start comparing it with my own childhood. I never used to fall ill so often. Even when Anuya talks about her aches and pains, I wonder why these two keep suffering from something or the other, while I always remain healthy.'

'You didn't need to fall sick, but perhaps Cheeku does. Whatever happened in your childhood was what you needed. Whatever happened with you is not happening with Cheeku, because your needs are different. We weigh everything on our own scales. We feel that if something did not happen to us, it should not happen to our spouse or our children. This is stamping.'

'Yes. That is the case with me.'

'Why should we think that what didn't happen to us shouldn't happen to others as well? Why do we want to create our clones? This desire only increases our suffering. You have tailored a jacket for Cheeku and now you want to fit him into that jacket, but he does not fit. This is the cause of your misery. You tell Cheeku to shed some fat here, add some fat there. As a result, you are unhappy and so is he. But you don't want to give up. You are determined to fit him into your jacket. You may try for years, but even then something or the other will not fit. Do you want to stay unhappy for many more years or do you agree that your jacket does not fit?'

'My jacket doesn't fit,' conceded Abhay.

'When you are able to see this clearly, you will simply throw away your jacket. If not, your love becomes an imposition on others. You think that you are doing things out of love, but your love becomes a torture for them. You want to make your child exactly like you. Please let your child develop the way he needs to. He is learning something. If falling sick is his need, just accept it. Investigate: do you want him to not fall sick because his sickness makes you suffer and is inconvenient for you?'

'I think you're right,' admitted Abhay, looking at the floor.

'Inner exploration will bring all this to your notice. Man says that if this loved one of mine was alive, I would've been happy. In other words, he doesn't even want to allow that individual to die—just to keep himself happy! Each person has come to earth for a purpose and will leave when his time is up. Let all that is coming come; let all that is going go. Investigate each suffering and find out your underlying stamping. If you feel miserable because the other person is ill, does that mean that he has no right to fall ill, just to make you happy?'

Abhay was listening to things he had never imagined. He was dumbstruck.

Hercules added, 'When things will become clear to you after the inner investigation, you will take all necessary precautions to keep Cheeku from falling sick, but you will not suffer. You will stop Cheeku from eating the things that make him sick, but you will not constantly fear the possibility of his falling sick. If you are fearful, your suffering will continue. When your investigation is complete, you will be free from this suffering.'

'I am very grateful to you for this invaluable guidance,' said Abhay.

'It's very late now. Let's go and rest,' Hercules said.

In the morning the priest woke up with a new thought. He decided, 'Now it's my turn to repent. Helping Hercules in his repentance will be my greatest repentance.' This new thought soothed him. He told Hercules, 'I want you to make a promise to me.'

'With pleasure! What do you want me to promise you?'

'After I get well, you will have to come back to the temple and stay with me—not to serve me, but to complete the rest of your tasks.'

'What does a blind man need? Two eyes!' said Hercules laughing.

The priest was relieved to hear this. He then asked, 'Who were you talking to in the corridor last night?'

'To Abhay. He wanted some guidance,' answered Hercules.

The priest said, 'I've been noticing that your clear counselling helps people solve their problems. Now that I'm here, you can counsel people in front of me so that I too may benefit from your wisdom.'

This request surprised Hercules. He thought, 'Why does he need any wisdom from me? He is a devotee of the Goddess. He has knowledge of all the scriptures and the holy books!' But he nodded.

In the few days that Hercules had been in the hospital, the other patients of the general ward had become aware of his wisdom. They used to talk to him and feel comforted. Hercules asked each patient to read the chapter 'Causes of Suffering: Stamping and Beliefs' from his magic book. Hercules knew the kinds of questions these people would ask him. He was already prepared for them.

Everyone was amazed to see a person who himself was a patient a few days ago now taking care of the priest. Even the doctors were taken aback.

Hercules helped the nurse with the priest's morning-care, such as medicines, sponging and breakfast. After the nurse left, Hercules relaxed and sat down. Just then, a middle-aged woman called Anupama Mukherji called out to Hercules from bed number 10 and said, 'Can I ask you a question?'

'Sure!' replied Hercules pleasantly and went and sat on a chair next to her.

'I am suffering from gastric ulcer. I am a Reiki master myself. I heal others keeping thoughts of well-being in mind. People benefit from my healing. But I feel bad. Why do I have this ailment? Despite doing good for others, why did this happen to me? I read the chapter you had marked for us, but I am unable to investigate the cause of my suffering,' said Anupama.

Hercules listened to her calmly and replied, 'First of all, you must understand that being a Reiki master or a healer does not mean that you will always remain free from diseases. Just because you heal others, it does not mean that you will always remain healthy. Second, you get diseases so that you know what disease is. Until you experience that yourself, you cannot really help others. Your illnesses are telling you something so that, in the future, you can help others better. Take this problem as an impersonal issue. If you consider it your illness, your suffering, then you will be troubled by it. Imagine that this disease has come to you so that you can learn about it and help others who are afflicted by it. Louis Kuhne, a pioneer of naturopathy, suffered from many illnesses since his childhood. His weakness and his ailments were the reason why he started researching and made great discoveries in the field of naturopathy. Your illness too can become instrumental in new discoveries that can benefit others.'

'Oh, is that so?' asked an astonished Anupama.

'Yes! You know what happened to Mahatma Gandhi. He was asked to get off the train at Pietermaritzburg Railway Station. Despite carrying a valid train ticket, he was abused, beaten up and thrown out of the train due to his race. Such injustice! However, this very injustice sparked the fire for freedom in him. He became instrumental in the freedom struggle that led to India gaining independence from British rule. He was treated like an untouchable in South Africa—that is why he became a champion for untouchables in India. These examples should tell you that your problems should not be considered personal. These problems have appeared in your life because, in the future, some great work needs to be done by you. Make these problems instrumental in acquiring and developing new qualities. Take full advantage of these problems. You'll spread health and happiness to many others. My good wishes are with you.'

Anupama was clearly moved by these words. She thanked him for these insights and started pondering over them. The priest had also been listening to Hercules. He too started mulling upon all that Hercules told Anupama. He had been suffering from a pain in the knee for the past two years. He used to wonder why the Goddess was making him suffer even though he was a priest at her temple. Today he had the answer to his question, at least partially.

After some time, the doctor came and examined the priest's leg. The swelling had subsided and so they decided to apply the plaster cast. He was taken to the operation theatre on a stretcher. After some manipulation, his leg was encased in a cast. When he was wheeled out of the operation theatre, the priest was groaning in pain. Hercules seemed like an angel standing by his side. He took the prescription from the doctor and also asked him how to administer the medicines. He then went and bought the medicines and after taking them, the priest fell asleep.

A middle-aged patient from bed number 3 softly beckoned Hercules.

His name was Mr Srinivasan. He wanted Hercules to solve one of his problems. Hercules agreed happily. Mr Srinivasan said, 'I've been meditating for many years now in order to experience self-realization, but my body is always afflicted by one disease or another which makes me dependent upon others. My diseases are becoming an obstacle in my spiritual growth. What is the solution for this? Can I achieve self-realization if I am dependent on others?'

Hercules replied, 'Physical diseases can never be an obstacle to spiritual growth. People who have attained the truth say that the body itself is a disease. That disease gets inflicted with another disease. They called the body a disease because the body makes us identify with it. However, when this body releases us from our attachment to it, then it doesn't remain a disease—it becomes a temple. Once you understand this, you will work towards repairing the temple. If the plaster or the paint of the temple needs some work, you will get down to it. This means that if there is suffering in your body, you will attempt to remove it. But if it doesn't leave, you will not sit and cry over it.'

'That's a radical thought! And it can prove to be very useful too,' said Mr Srinivasan.

'Ancient saints have gone to the extent of saying, "It is important to have physical pain so that you remember the truth. Otherwise, man gets absorbed in his comforts and forgets God." If you can learn to use your pain in the right way, it will remind you of the real thing hidden behind your pain. Which means it will remind you that you are the self, not the body. The pain is occurring to your body and not to you. If you can do this, the disease will prove beneficial to you.'

'Is that so?'

'Indeed! There is nothing in this world that can become an obstacle in the attainment of truth. An illness is not an obstacle but it can seem like one. No hell has been created by the creator, but you can experience one if you so desire. People can experience hell due to their beliefs. But the fact remains that there is no hell. Likewise, disease is not an impediment to spiritual progress. This does not imply that you don't have to get yourself treated. You must get the best treatment. But if some disease is incurable, make it a medium for your growth. When your illness keeps reminding you of your real self, that illness is beneficial. Make your disease a medium for self-realization. Understand that self-realization can be achieved in spite of illnesses.'

'That's quite reassuring. I feel good about it now,' said Mr Srinivasan.

Hercules continued, 'Now let us take up your second question: is there any connection between self-realization and dependence upon others? Let us understand it this way. When you want to go somewhere to learn spiritual practices for training your mind, you need to depend upon others for travelling due to your physical condition. But you do not need to take help or permission from your family members, relatives or neighbours in order to contemplate. Unconditional bliss is our basic nature. Dependence upon others does not stop us from enjoying this bliss. It is the limitation of your body that it is dependent upon others, Mr Srinivasan. Make this limitation a challenge, but not a stumbling block.'

'You have given me new perspective. It will help me a lot,' said Mr Srinivasan.

Words were flowing from Hercules' mouth. He went on, 'When you play carrom, you follow the rule of placing the striker between the two lines on the carrom board. We easily follow this rule while playing, but when it comes to playing the game of life we protest, 'How can we live between two lines? It is impossible.' You need to lead your life while living between the two lines of the body and mind. Even if you are physically dependent on others, you need to express your true self while staying within this limitation. If a child tells you that he is unable to play while staying between the two lines of the carrom board, you will say, "It will come with practice." After practicing, the child's opinion will change. He will say, "Now I can play while staying between the two lines. You can place the carrom-men anywhere and I will be able to pocket them."'

'This is profound!' said Mr Srinivasan.

Hercules continued to speak as though an invisible force was inspiring him. 'Similarly, when your practice is complete, when your contemplation is complete, you will remain immersed in the bliss of your being under all circumstances. There is no need for us to depend upon others for our happiness. The limitations that have been placed upon you are your challenges. Learn to look at each limitation as a challenge. Always keep the example of the carrom board in your mind. Those two lines have been drawn for nothing but your benefit. If the lines were erased and you were asked to play, you would say that there was no enjoyment left in the game. Therefore, understand the rules of this game called life. Practise in the right manner and play successfully.'

Mr Srinivasan said that he had never heard such a brilliant exposition. Hercules told Mr Srinivasan that it was time to rest and, marvelling at his own answers, he went off for a little walk.

In the evening, all the patients of the general ward got together at tea time and started talking about Hercules. Those who had heard him speak told the others about his wisdom. They all decided to do some reading each day and in the evening, after tea, ask Hercules to throw some light on their questions.

The priest took *The Path to Peace* and read the chapter on the causes of suffering. He understood the meaning of stamping, repeat order for suffering, beliefs, etc. and started drawing parallels with his own life.

As decided, after the afternoon siesta the next day, all the patients gathered around the priest's and Cheeku's bed. They requested Hercules to speak about the root causes of disease in detail.

Hercules was ready with his book. He bowed to it in respect and started reading.

> Today we will learn how our thoughts are the cause of our diseases. Feelings that arise in our mind bring about chemical changes in our body and produce diseases. A person who harbours jealousy, anger, fear, worry, stress and malice cannot digest his food properly. Deceit of any kind produces diseases of the alimentary system. Man wants to hide these mental vices from others in order to maintain his image in society. This habit makes his body weak and sick.

Some people sat up straight as though Hercules was referring to them.

> These vices play a primary role in aggravating diseases. Excessive anger and irritation damage the liver and the gallbladder. Fear causes harm to the kidneys and the urinary bladder. Stress and worry impair the pancreas. Impatience and impulsiveness weaken the heart and the small intestine. Grief reduces the capacity of the lungs and the large intestine. People who think too much do not feel like sharing things with anyone. This habit of miserliness hampers their bowels from excreting stool, their skin from expelling sweat and their lungs from exhaling air.

Everyone started thinking about their vices. They realized that if they did not keep them in check, they would fall prey to corresponding ailments in the future.

We can take care of our health through positive thoughts. We should not feel belittled even when we are insulted. Negative thoughts invite diseases and produce more ailments. The poor body has to suffer the brunt. Therefore do not repeat negative thoughts. Instead, choose positive thoughts.

'This means that our health is in our own hands. We are responsible for our well-being,' Abhay said.

'Exactly!' said Hercules, and resumed reading.

People who harbour hatred and malice invite diseases of the heart and stomach. Often a heart attack is just an outer manifestation of a 'hate attack' or 'head attack' (an attack of thoughts) inside. A mind full of worries can even make a person insane. The poison of worry seeps in gradually and makes a person's body the dwelling place of diseases. Negative thoughts drain away all enthusiasm from life. This makes one depressed and hopeless. Such a person gives up the will to live. When someone gives up the will to live, he takes a long time to get well. But those who have a strong hope for life and a desire to live recover very quickly.

Those who have an aim in life, those who have involved themselves in some powerful mission, those whose minds are full of creative and constructive thoughts have an intense desire to live. They can overcome any serious disease. Keep this flame of hope burning in your hearts. While eating your food, remember that you are eating to stay healthy and to gain the cooperation of your body in achieving your goals. When you do this, you will eat no more than what is required. You will keep a check on your taste buds and eat the right food, exercise regularly and rest as required.

Anger and stress create tension in your nerves, which leads

to aches and pains. Stress can last from three hours to three days. When we cultivate the feeling of acceptance in our minds, our stress begins to reduce. Otherwise we need to keep taking sedatives for a long time. You may definitely make use of medicines, but do not forget to eliminate the root cause of stress. The moment thoughts of fear and doubt appear in our minds, our energy is sucked out and we feel weak. Fearful thoughts are the enemy of self-confidence. Fear and doubt stop man from doing the things he has come to do on this planet. Always keep your mind full of positive and happy thoughts. Start working towards a healthy mind and see its effect on your body. Don't ever let hope, acceptance and happiness diminish. If you accomplish this, you will gain total health, i.e. health in all five aspects of life: physical, mental, social, financial and spiritual.

After listening to this chapter, everyone's face was shining with joy. Gayatri Devi of bed number 6 was also sitting amongst them. She belonged to a royal family and possessed a composed and serious disposition. She used to listen to Hercules attentively and silently. She had not spoken about herself until now, but she was always present when anyone shared anything with Hercules. Today, she couldn't stop herself. She heard about the root causes of illness and started sobbing. Everyone fell silent.

She collected herself and began, 'I am a married woman of royal origin, though our family does not enjoy the same status and power as before. Even our economic condition is going from bad to worse. I want to tell you all about the mental condition of a woman who grows up in such circumstances. I have been leading a stressful life since childhood. We royals have to take care of our image, pride and respect to such an extent that our true identity gets lost. We live a pretentious life. We suppress our minds and invite many diseases. This is what has happened to me. But now I can't take it any more. I want to live a free life. Today, after listening to you, I have understood that all the vices that you mentioned have been present in me. As a result, I am suffering from a whole lot of diseases. The farce of maintaining a good image invites illness. Now, I wish to let go of all pretension.'

Hercules empathized with her saying, 'Your unhesitant disclosure is itself the beginning of a free life. You must continue your contemplation in writing. Freedom is not far from you.'

After some time, the doctor came for his evening rounds. He was pleasantly surprised to see them all sitting and laughing together. On his arrival, they dispersed and went to their respective beds. The doctor noticed a positive change in all of them. After the doctor left, Hercules asked them all to practise recognizing the vices they harboured in their minds.

Collective reading and Hercules' interpretation brought about a positive change—the focus of all the patients had shifted from their illnesses to self-investigation. They started reflecting upon how diseases can be a blessing. They realized that there are many causes of disease and that we look at only one side of the story and become unhappy. The general ward, which earlier used to be full of moans and groans, was now filled with silent contemplation. The patients were investigating their own internal worlds. Some contemplated in writing, while some did it with eyes closed.

The next afternoon when the patients gathered together, their faces were glowing. Mrs Manjeet Kaur from bed number 5 and her daughter Mandira were also present. Mrs Manjeet Kaur had been operated upon for appendicitis. Her daughter was taking care of her. Mandira was somewhat anxious. She started the conversation, 'God has fulfilled all my prayers, but my prayer of becoming a mother has not been answered. This makes me very sad.'

Hercules said, 'This prayer of yours has also been answered.'

Mandira looked at him askance.

'Yes, you are your own first child. First prove that you can look after it. Love that child and prepare her completely. Then see what happens.'

'I haven't understood anything!'

'This world has given us a lot of beliefs. These beliefs make us unhappy and cause suffering. We can come out of this only after investigating deep within.'

'People keep taunting me, saying I'm barren. I feel very hurt,' Mandira said.

'This is their belief. Don't give undue importance to their beliefs. People can say anything out of ignorance. In reality, they all live in fear. When a person does something which is different from the established norms, they feel as if they themselves are wrong. Therefore, in order to prove themselves right, they start belittling others. This is their problem, born out of ignorance. Just as sick people start becoming irritable, similarly ignorant people start blabbering. You listen to their blabbering and start believing in it. This is the beginning of your suffering.

'Man believes that he becomes complete only when he has children. This happens because man considers himself to be the body. But the reality is that man feels complete only when he returns to his true self, his essence. First try to achieve that completeness. In addition, just find out what is happening to people who have children.'

Mandira replied, 'I know that just having a child does not fulfil a person. Even those who have children end up living alone. But we have been programmed since childhood that a woman achieves fulfilment only on becoming a mother. This belief refuses to leave me.'

Hercules said, 'Man feels incomplete because he considers his body to be him. When you will know yourself to be beyond the body, the feeling of being incomplete will never arise because you are already complete. Nothing can be taken away from completeness and nothing can be added to completeness. Completeness is just that—complete. Nothing less, nothing more. Many infertile women are spending their lives in despondency, but you need to live with understanding. Do not think that only a child can make you complete. The reality is something else. Ask yourself, 'What should I do to live a better life? Does my infertility mean that I cannot live a complete life? I haven't got a child, so has my life come to a standstill?' Life never stops. Besides, everyone in this world is not meant to do the same job. Some people discover new paths to walk on. They become an inspiration for others. People look at these happy souls and think that they too can lead their life in that manner. When you walk on a new path, such issues stop bothering you. The divine possibility of every human being opens up.'

'That would be great. But it's easier said than done.'

'Agreed. But it's definitely worth trying! We tend to satisfy ourselves with very small possibilities. A woman gives birth to a child and feels that her life is fulfilled! The truth is that the body has just done its job—that was its role. Those who do not have a child should ask themselves if they want to make this issue a boon or a bane. There is another belief regarding children which must be broken. Women think that only if a child is born from their own womb it is their child. If you let go of this belief, then you will have so many children to love. You can take any child and love him or her. Who's to stop you?'

'I agree with that.'

'First, become your own child. Start loving this child. It will open a new dimension for you. Otherwise, you will keep waiting for a child to be born to you so that you get an opportunity to love! First start loving yourself. Prove yourself to be your own best parent. And if you still want a child, you can adopt one. Today, science has made great advances and many new methods of having a child have opened up. But please remember that your life does not stop just because you do not have a child. You need to decide whether you want to spend your life happily or sadly. If you do not contemplate on this, or if you give too much importance to what others say, then there is nothing but suffering for you.'

Mandira fell into deep thought.

'Now start paying more attention to the thoughts emanating from the source within you. If you love the truth, you will give more importance to thoughts of truth. If you love the truth, there is no problem. Otherwise every thought and everything is a problem. Now, whenever you get the thought, 'I don't have a baby,' just say, 'I'm here!' Then love yourself and take good care of yourself. Doing this will open a new door for you. You will feel joyful. Your so-called curse will become a blessing. Learn the art of converting each problem into a boon. You have to become such a philosopher's stone that, by staying with you, others become not just gold but another philosopher's stone. You have to become such a person who not only changes her thoughts, but is an inspiration for others to change theirs.'

Mrs Manjeet Kaur said, 'I agree with you, but my daughter's in-laws and other relatives feel that she should have a child. I feel that along with her, her family should also be happy.'

'Is it guaranteed that after the birth of a child her family will be happy? There are so many women who have children—are their in-laws happy?'

'No, there is no guarantee.'

'That is why you have to do two things: first, you have to investigate within and stay happy. And second, you have to leave everything to god. The label "my daughter" is coming in the way of your happiness. It is making you miserable. Ask yourself, "Will Mandira's in-laws be permanently happy if she has a child?" Everyone thinks differently and everyone has a different life. When you attain clarity on this subject, you should have a dialogue with your daughter and her in-laws with a clear perspective and accept whatever happens after that.'

'We are grateful to you for giving us such valuable knowledge and advice. Until now, we were looking at this problem through our limited perspective. You have broadened our outlook,' said Mandira and Mrs Manjeet Kaur.

'My pleasure! It's getting late now. The doctor is about to come on his evening rounds. We shall share the essence of our contemplation tomorrow,' said Hercules.

The priest, hearing Hercules talk about the importance of investigating within, turned inwards. He started analysing his own life.

- I was planning to put a spoke in the wheels of Hercules' penance. Did that cause my accident?
- If this accident had not occurred, would I have known Hercules in the real sense?
- If this accident had not occurred, I don't think I would have listened to Hercules imparting such higher knowledge.

- Speaking to other patients has helped increase my own understanding.

- I used to advise all the devotees and preach wisdom, but I remained the same. Perhaps this event has occurred to make me experience that wisdom.

- This accident has been instrumental in opening my eyes. So how can I call it a bad event?

- Whatever happens to us happens because it is what we need at that time.

The doctor examined the priest's leg and changed the dressings of his other bruises. Today all the patients were silent, as opposed to yesterday. The doctor asked why and the priest replied, 'One feels real happiness only after returning from silence.' The doctor couldn't understand this answer but he noticed that all the patients looked serene and content. All of them were enquiring into their own illnesses. Everyone wanted to get out of their miserable mind-set as soon as possible.

The doctor informed the priest that he would be discharged the next day. This made the atmosphere both happy and sad. The patients did not want to let Hercules go. They decided to complete their investigation by the next afternoon and share it with each other, however long it took.

Abhay and Anuya sat together and investigated through Cheeku's illness. Anupama Mukherji, who used to heal others through Reiki, started investigating through her ailment. Mrs Manjeet Kaur and her daughter Mandira were jointly exploring the subject of infertility. The priest was analysing his dark and corrupt ways and wondering if there was a link with his accident. Mr Srinivasan, who had been involved in spiritual practices for many years, was searching for the final truth.

By now, Cheeku's health had improved a lot. He said sweetly, 'Uncle Hercules, I also want to tell you the cause of my unhappiness.'

'Sure, son. Tell me,' said Hercules while the others stared in astonishment.

Cheeku began, 'When my parents fight with each other, I feel very bad. I do not feel sad about my sickness, but I feel sad when my parents worry over my sickness. If I accidentally break something and my mother scolds me, I feel like crying. When I do not score well in my examinations and my parents scold me, I feel horrible.'

Hercules lovingly sat Cheeku on his lap and gave him a chocolate. His words made everyone think of the suffering little children undergo because of the behaviour of adults. Now that they had received this understanding, they understood the harm that unhappiness causes and the importance of awareness in such cases.

Hercules was happy that he had been admitted to the hospital, due to which he was able to impart this priceless knowledge to so many people. During this time, he was able to conduct a deep investigation into his own health as well. His belief that everything happens for the good was validated.

Until now, Hercules had been under the impression that he could carry out his penance by way of the tasks assigned by the priest. But the priest had not sent him to the hospital and yet he felt as though it had been a task given by the priest. He realized that it is actually God who makes us do everything. We give different labels to it. Even the tasks given by the priest were actually part of the larger divine plan. A new meaning of life manifested before him.

It was time for Hercules and the priest to leave. Everyone felt sad. They wanted to stay in touch with Hercules. He told them about his abode atop the hill and asked them to visit him after being discharged from the hospital. At the same time, he presented a copy of *The Path to Peace* to each of them. Abhay and Anuya said on behalf of everyone that they would all visit hospitals in their respective areas in order to conduct readings of the book for the benefit of other patients.

Hercules and the priest took their leave and reached the temple. On opening the doors, they saw some letters waiting for them. Besides the usual donations and bills, there was a letter for the priest. When he opened the letter and read it, he was ecstatic. A reputed and cultured family from the neighbouring village had asked for his daughter's hand in marriage for their son. The priest felt as though things were starting to fall in place.

The doctor had said that the cast had to remain in place for at least six weeks. Hercules served him with great devotion during this period. At the same time, he shouldered all the responsibilities of the temple and its upkeep. He started solving the devotees' problems after the evening prayers and advised them to be happy all the time, no matter what. He began to feel that his real self—the self—had awakened.

Now Hercules was waiting for the priest's next order. He still had to free four people from suffering in the next four months.

SIX
The Fifth Task of Hercules: Herding in the Cattle —Investigating Thoughts

The daily routine at the temple continued, albeit with a difference. The priest was in a dilemma. He was feeling guilty and his thoughts were at war with one another. Even though the cast had been removed and his leg had gotten better, he still hadn't resumed his duties at the temple under the pretext of weakness and spent most of his time in solitude. Meanwhile, Hercules was happily carrying out all the activities such as conducting prayers and rituals, cleaning the temple, guiding the devotees and so on.

The priest was engrossed in investigating within himself. He had decided to stop all his illegal activities and to find real joy and devotion by strengthening the foundation of his thoughts. After a great amount of deliberation he determined that as soon as Hercules went away for a few days, he would wipe out all evidence of his ill deeds and start life afresh. This resolve put him at ease. He slept peacefully after a long time.

In the morning the priest entered the temple with a newfound joy. He saw a well-to-do gentleman entering the temple with a platter of offerings. The man handed over the platter to Hercules and asked him to offer it to the Goddess. As he turned around after offering his prayers, he saw the priest and exclaimed, 'Greetings! Do you recognize me?'

The priest looked at him. He mumbled, 'Are you Parimal?'

'You're right! I'm Parimal Dave.'

'You've changed a lot! You used to be quite skinny. It's been a long time since I last saw you. Where have you been all these years?' the priest asked.

'Wherever I was, I always remembered you. I'm leading a prosperous life today and the credit goes to you!'

'This is the blessing of the Goddess,' replied the priest.

Parimal belonged to the village. Until a few years ago, he was a frequent visitor to the temple. After completing his education he decided to go to Mauritius for business, but he was apprehensive of living in a foreign land. He also wondered whether he would be successful. He was quite anxious about it all. That is when he had sought advice from the priest. The priest had encouraged him, 'Have faith and devotion for the Goddess. Work with dedication and passion. You will surely succeed. And when you achieve success, do not forget the grace of the Goddess.' Thanks to these encouraging words and the blessings of the Goddess, Parimal had become a successful businessman and a respected citizen of Mauritius.

Parimal said, 'I have built a temple in Mauritius. I want you to come and establish the statue of the Goddess in it. I have come to invite you for that. I also want to make a small donation to this temple. I'll arrange your travel and stay in Mauritius, as well as the passport and visa.'

The priest replied, 'That's wonderful! You've come from so far—rest here awhile, and in the evening make full use of the guidance provided by the Goddess' special devotee, Hercules. After giving some thought to your proposal, we'll take a decision in the morning.' The priest asked Hercules to make arrangements for Parimal's stay.

Parimal was impressed by Hercules' personality and humility. In the evening, Hercules solved the problems of people who visited the temple. Seeing this, Parimal's respect for Hercules grew even more. On the other hand, the priest was thinking, 'This is a golden opportunity. I will send Hercules with Parimal and in the meantime, I shall destroy all evidence of my evil deeds and dispose of all the narcotics. Hercules won't have a clue. Then I will begin my life afresh with self-respect and a clean conscience. Only then will I be worthy of all the respect that is showered upon me here in the temple.'

The next day, the priest expressed his inability to go to Mauritius. He cited his poor health. He offered to send Hercules in his place. Parimal readily agreed to this. He had already made a sketchy outline of the entire visit to Mauritius. Now he finalized it after discussing it with Hercules. The day Hercules reached Mauritius, the temple would be inaugurated. Then there would be a community lunch, followed by Hercules' address. The next three days were reserved for sightseeing and meeting with important people. Parimal took leave from them to take care of all the formalities and returned home to prepare for Hercules' visit.

After a few days, when all the travel formalities had been completed, Hercules took permission from the priest to leave. In the afternoon, he left for the airport and reached there by late evening. He had a late night flight. In the meantime, he started looking around the bustling airport. The shops displayed the latest goods. Bright lights, neon signs and the latest electronic gadgets were everywhere. He took his boarding pass and went through the security check. Now all he had to do was wait for the boarding call. Every few minutes, he would observe some aircraft landing or taking off. Various airlines were making their announcements, while their staff was busy with various activities. Hercules thought, 'On one hand, science has made so many inventions, and on the other, man is caught in the blind rat race of materialistic luxuries and personal aspirations. The truth of life has fallen behind. No one feels the need for internal exploration or growth.'

His flight was announced and Hercules boarded the plane and took his seat. He had a window seat and was happy that he could enjoy the view. As he was fastening his seatbelt, a middle-aged woman came and took the seat next to him. She smiled and said, 'Hello,' which Hercules acknowledged with a nod. As soon as the airhostess finished with the safety instructions and other announcements, the plane took off and soared into the sky. Hercules unfastened his seat belt, wiped his face with a cold towel and sipped on some juice. His fellow passenger initiated a conversation saying, 'My name is Charusheela. I am Indian, but I've been living in Mauritius for many years. I had come to India to attend a wedding. There are many Indian families in Mauritius. We all live in perfect harmony. From time to time, we organize various programmes. The day after tomorrow, we are organizing a self-development workshop titled Journey of Growth. I have been given the responsibility to host it.' Hercules too introduced himself and told her the reason for his visit to Mauritius.

They both weren't really tired and so they kept talking for a long time. Charusheela was impressed with Hercules' thoughts and his manner of speaking. She was also very enthusiastic about the workshop. She said, 'In this workshop, the participants will learn how to deal with the problems they face at the level of thought. The purpose is to make them mentally stronger and bring about a positive change in their thinking. The internationally renowned psychologist, Dr David, is the chief guest and will be providing us guidance on this subject.' Their conversation continued for some more time, after which they fell asleep.

At the crack of dawn, Hercules woke up and looked outside his window. The sky seemed like a bright canvas. The sun was peeking over the horizon. The white clouds below looked like tufts of cotton. Hercules was immersed in this breath-taking scene when the air hostess announced the landing and requested the passengers to fasten their seatbelts and straighten the back of their chairs. After a short while, the aircraft went below the white clouds and Hercules could see land again. Hills, bushes, the sea, winding rivers, roads, buildings, gardens—everything could be seen clearly. He remembered a sentence from *The Path to Peace*. It said, 'Never make assumptions after seeing just one aspect. When you take a bird's eye view of things, you will be able to clearly see all the aspects together and get the full picture.' Seeing the entire scene at once made him smile.

Charusheela asked him the reason for his smile and he told her how we tend to look at events in life from inside a little well and feel unhappy, when we ought to be taking a bird's eye view to understand the larger plan. To demonstrate this point, he pointed towards a train that could be seen through the window. 'Look at that train running on those winding tracks. Only a part of it can be seen at a time when you look at it from the station. But it extends way beyond your view. Similarly, a river originates in the high mountains and follows a winding path through high and low areas, but people can't see its full length. For them, the length of the river is what they can see. But when we look at it from above, the reality emerges. This is true about life as well. We look at life through our narrow views. In reality, there is more to life than we can see.'

Charusheela was already impressed with Hercules, but now she was becoming his fan. She asked, 'Can you make some time to present your views on life during our workshop?'

Hercules replied, 'Why not? If I can spare some time from my schedule, I will definitely come.'

At the airport, Hercules promised Charusheela that he would try his best and took leave from her. Parimal was waiting with his friends to welcome Hercules. He then took Hercules to a luxurious guest house. After Hercules had freshened up and relaxed for a while, they got ready and left for the temple. The temple was inaugurated amidst great festivity. Hercules interacted with the devotees and participated in the community lunch. His discourse was scheduled for the evening.

Charusheela had to supervise all the arrangements for the workshop. Therefore, she headed straight to the corporate centre where the workshop was to be organized. The corporate centre was an ultra-modern structure spread over a large area. There were beautiful gardens surrounding the building. One had to walk down a long pathway before reaching the main entrance. This path was lined on both sides by flagpoles representing every country. The main hall was air-conditioned and soundproof. It had a seating capacity of 1,000. The large stage had a semi-circular, silver-coloured dais with an attractive flower arrangement. On the right side of the main hall, arrangements had been made for refreshments. On the left side was another hall earmarked for group discussions.

While Charusheela and the other members of the organizing committee were inspecting the arrangements, they received the news that Dr David, who was to arrive that evening, would be unable to come due to a small accident. Charusheela was dumbstruck. Who would conduct the workshop now? Who would be the main speaker? What would happen? Everyone seemed lost. Nobody knew what to do. Suddenly, Charusheela remembered Hercules and her conversation with him during the flight. His charming personality and enlightened thoughts made him amply qualified to conduct the workshop. She consulted with the other members and they all left this decision to her judgement.

Charusheela took a couple of members with her and turned up at the temple. Hercules' discourse was nearing completion. The way Hercules summarized his entire discourse made Charusheela bow her head in respect. After the crowd thinned out, she approached Hercules and greeted him. She explained the situation to him and requested him to guide them in the workshop. Since Hercules had come to Mauritius on Parimal's invitation, and he had prepared the schedule and made all the arrangements, Hercules spoke to him about the matter. Parimal realized that the situation was critical and allowed Hercules to participate in the workshop. A happy and reassured Charusheela told Hercules that she would pick him up at 11 a.m.

Hercules was feeling tired after his journey and the hectic day, so he went off to sleep early. The next morning, he woke up earlier than usual. Feeling rested and refreshed, he opened *The Path to Peace* and started reading. At eleven, he was ready to leave with Charusheela for the corporate centre.

The workshop began on time. Almost all the invitees were present. Charusheela introduced Hercules briefly and invited him to present his thoughts and guide the audience.

Hercules began by speaking about the importance of staying happy and of searching for happiness. He apprised them in detail about the meaning of inner investigation, the importance of investigating problems from all angles, the technique of investigation, the significance of refraining from stamping and manufacturing stories about people and events.

Since the workshop centred on giving direction to thoughts, Hercules took the help of an analogy. He said, 'There was a village in which everybody used to walk on their hands, upside down, with their feet in the air. That was the way all of them lived. You can imagine how difficult it must have been for them to work. Every activity took much more time and effort than normal.

'Once, a person who walked upright visited the village. He was a normal person. He looked at all the people and asked them, "Why are you walking like this? This must be making it so difficult for you to work! You must be taking a lot more time and spending a lot more energy to do the simplest things. Your efficiency and quality must be quite low!"

'The villagers had no idea that they took longer or spent more energy to do their work. They told him to prove his statement. The upright person said, 'Fine. I'll prove it. Tell me, what all do you do in a day?' When the villagers told him about all the activities they carried out, he completed all of them much sooner. The villagers watched with their mouths agape. Looking at the speed and efficiency with which he worked, they believed him. They then beseeched him to train them so that they too could work like him. The upright person imparted the appropriate training and straightened them all up. The villagers thanked him for turning everyone upside down—their definition of upside down itself was upside down! They considered their original position to be upright.

'Similarly, when you are being asked to look at thoughts of unhappiness upside down, you are actually being asked to look at things upright. For example, if you habitually think that the world is full of cheats, you should now ponder on the question, "Am I a cheat too? Am I cheating myself?" This kind of thinking is called upright thinking, which is also known as inner investigation.

'If you have been cheating others and are being cheated by others, you will consider everyone in the world a cheat. You never realize that you are cheating others. But now you have to become an investigator and investigate your own thoughts. An investigator has a unique way of working. When he starts his investigation into who is the murderer or the thief, he investigates every person, he investigates from all angles. That is what you have to do.'

After the first part of the lecture was over, Charusheela announced, 'Now it's time for lunch and a contemplation break. Everyone please move into the group discussion hall to reflect upon all that has been said and to discuss amongst each other. You may then have your lunch and return to this hall in an hour.'

The afternoon session began after lunch. Hercules asked the audience to share any questions that might have arisen after their reflection.

A lady had a question. She said, 'I really like all that you have said about inner investigation. Now I will investigate every aspect of every thing that causes me suffering or unhappiness. But I have a problem. Whenever I start something good, something or the other happens to make me leave that work halfway. Now I have lost the will to do anything new.'

Hercules said, 'It may have happened to you before, but please do not stamp it with the belief that it will happen in future as well…'

'But it has happened so many times,' protested the woman.

'True. But if you stamp an event, you allow it to happen again. Thus, you keep receiving proofs for your belief. Now you have to pedal your cycle in the opposite direction—which is actually the right direction. When you stamp on your thoughts, assumptions, beliefs and stories and start considering them to be the truth, then those thoughts become even more painful. Because you think you are right, you keep thinking those thoughts. Thus, your negative thoughts multiply. If you do not investigate your thoughts and keep stamping on them throughout the day, your suffering will increase.

'Now, to begin with, start investigating those beliefs and stories that make you unhappiest. When those sorrows are resolved, turn your attention to the thoughts that subtly trouble you. Do not spare any belief, big or small. Throughout the day, you have to monitor your thoughts and catch those that take you far away from reality. You need to investigate them. After you do this, you will save a lot of time—which you used to spend thinking useless thoughts—and you will be able to utilize it constructively. You will become more creative and you will start getting more thoughts that take you towards your true self. You should be aware of all the energy that you waste in meaningless thoughts, and learn how to save that energy and use it for creative work. Only a sensible and happy person can think in this manner. Such thinking benefits not just that person but the entire society, the country—and even the world.'

The lady found the explanation satisfactory.

Next, an old lady spoke up. 'As it is, I am always absorbed in thought. I am afraid of getting more entangled while investigating them.'

Hercules said, 'No, that is not how it works. In fact, it is exactly the opposite. When useless thoughts stop appearing, the mind becomes silent and you start becoming an observer, a witness. Then you start waiting for thoughts. Whenever you begin to observe your thoughts as a witness, they disappear. At that time, you feel that you don't have to do anything—all you have to do is observe. This awakens the observer or witness within you. It is this state that takes you towards your centre or the self. Therefore, please understand that investigation gives your thoughts the right direction. Where negative thoughts end, happy thoughts begin. Happy thoughts purify the mind. A pure mind takes you to a thoughtless state. And a thoughtless state takes you towards self-realization.'

Several participants asked, 'We want to become positive thinkers, but negative thoughts keep appearing in our minds. What should we do?'

Hercules said, 'For that, you will need to maintain constant awareness. We will discuss this topic in detail after tea.'

After the tea break, Hercules talked about the importance of becoming a positive thinker.

'To become a positive thinker, you need to maintain constant awareness. You need to do each of your tasks with awareness. If someone hurts you or doesn't do something according to your expectations, you must be alert lest you lose your temper and start cursing him or yourself. A cycle of negative thoughts begins in this way. Therefore, you need to learn to see the positive aspects of negative events. This will keep you aware, always.

'Let us first understand how people lose their awareness. Television and newspapers are the main culprits. People watch TV and keep absorbing new beliefs every day. They watch and read news about violence, thefts, riots, lawlessness, etc. which makes them feel that the world is deteriorating. But that is not so. Your inner exploration will tell you that you are deteriorating because your attention is only on negative things. The world has always been like this. There have always been people like Dhritarashtra and Duryodhana—the villains of the Mahabharata. The only difference is that these days, the news reaches you within seconds. If you explore in the right direction and look at people from a new perspective, people too will change. The interesting part is that people don't change because you don't learn. Earlier you used to think, 'I am unhappy because people are bad.' After your investigation, you will realize that people have to keep playing negative roles in your life because you are not learning.'

There was some movement in the audience.

Hercules continued, 'When you learn what your role is, the other person's negative role will end. It is like someone coming to you every day to remind you of something. If you don't remember it, that person will keep coming back even though you resent him. But the day you learn it, he won't need to come and remind you any more. His negative role will end. Similarly, nature too tries to teach you something through events. This is the great arrangement made in our life.'

Now there were some murmurs in the audience.

'You hear all kinds of news on TV and you share it with others. Negative news triggers a feeling of fear inside you. You start thinking, 'I hope this doesn't happen to me.' In this way, negative news has a negative impact on you. If you are not aware, then within a few years your entire thought process will become negative. You will look at everyone with suspicion. Everyone will look red through your red glasses—the glasses of your beliefs. Therefore, people will seem bad to you. How can you live in peace under such conditions?'

There was a hush in the auditorium.

'You will wonder how it is possible to live in peace and joy in this world, amongst its people. Your mind will give you enough proof for your belief that people have become bad, politicians have become corrupt, civil servants have become inefficient, everyone's thinking has become sick, there is violence everywhere... Then how can you be happy? This type of thinking is proof of a deep-seated ignorance. When you investigate within, in the right manner, you will come to know that you were looking at the world through the glasses of your beliefs. And because you are unaware, all the treatments that you employ to relieve your suffering will prove to be temporary. These temporary measures do not make you happy. Instead, they make you more miserable. For example: If you have fought with a relative, you stop talking to him. This action benefits you in the short term, but later you end up having a bigger fight and everything becomes more complicated instead of getting resolved. By stopping communication, you actually start preparing for war. This preparation does take some time. Investigate within yourself during that time. Ask yourself whether you should feel unhappy and torment yourself, or whether you should remain happy and positive.'

A gentleman in the audience asked, 'Should we go to the seclusion of the Himalayas to explore within ourselves?'

Hercules answered, 'You have come to earth so that you can train amongst people. If you sit in the Himalayas, never come down among people and then pass away, then what was the point of coming to earth? You may go to the Himalayas for vacations—that's fine. But if you start living there, how will you realize your complete possibility as a human being? Only when you come down from your high abode will you get a chance to explore within! Only then will you be able to view each event in a different light. When you see nature's wonderful arrangement from the right perspective, you will start appreciating the very things you used to find ugly. If you apply makeup on yourself in this way, you will find yourself looking more beautiful. When you see yourself as beautiful, the world around you becomes beautiful, too. The world, after all, is a reflection of who you are and what you believe in. The world is your mirror. By makeup, I do not mean applying cream or lipstick; makeup implies—investigating within through contemplation, and increasing understanding through awareness. Right now, as you are listening to these words, you are applying makeup.'

Someone spoke up from a corner, 'You said that in order to become a positive thinker you have to maintain constant awareness and apply makeup. I like this concept. My problem is that when things don't happen according to my wish, I feel a resistance towards them.

This resistance makes it difficult for me to stay aware. What can I do at such times?'

Hercules replied, 'In order to get rid of your resistance, first start liking what you don't like. And always remember that whatever is happening with you is exactly what you need at that moment. This understanding helps destroy the resistance inside you. As a result, your attention is free to concentrate on what you need at that moment and, thereby, attract it. If you feel resentment towards something and keep fighting with your negative feelings, you will need to stay in the boxing ring with it. Therefore, let go of negativity and sow the seeds of positivity. Otherwise, you will keep thinking of negative things and let them enter your life. Tell me, who do you remember more, friends or foes?'

A woman from the front row replied, 'Foes.'

'That's right. You hardly think about people with whom you have cordial relations, while you often think about those you hate. If you start liking your foes, you will soon be liberated from negative emotions. If you dislike them, you will be stuck with your negative emotions. This is how the mind works. If you lose a tooth, your tongue automatically keeps going to that vacant spot. When you start liking the fact that you have a tooth missing, you will stop thinking about it. Liking something means accepting it as it is. Then you will not feel resentment towards it or feel unhappy about it. Whatever you accept, you do not think too much about. Acceptance releases you from suffering. If you hate something, your mind will keep going there. Liking an event doesn't mean that you will not try to find a solution or will not visit the doctor if you are ill. It means that you will get rid of your resistance towards it so that it can easily dissolve.'

Another woman said, 'My mind keeps going to the future—that is why I cannot maintain awareness.'

Hercules said, 'Whatever is happening in the present will give you awareness and bring about a permanent transformation, or shifting, in your thought process. What has not yet happened cannot make you aware. It is just in your imagination. Daydreaming cannot help you stabilize in your true Self. Only what is happening now can give you self-stabilization. If hatred makes you feel negative and you keep resisting it, you will attract more hatred. It is a law of nature—whatever you resist, persists. If someone has abused you, just accept that the abuse was a need of the moment. You do not need to keep thinking about the person who abused you. Instead, you have to work towards attracting love into your life. You may pray and sow this seed: Let there be an abundance of love and joy in my life.'

At that moment, Charusheela came in and announced the start of a Q & A session.

People handed over their questions to Hercules. Hercules read them and realized that people were trapped in their wrong beliefs to such an extent that it was almost impossible for them to come out. Therefore, he decided to shed some light on the source of thoughts and teach them how to untangle the mess of thoughts through investigation. He began:

'Man is very gullible. He loses himself in his own web of illusions and fails to see his real self. For example, if a person takes a few audio recorders, records different dialogues in each of them, and plays them back all at once, it would seem like a group of people are talking to each other—someone is asking questions, someone is answering. Anybody sitting outside the room would think that there are many people sitting inside discussing their woes. But when he goes in he will realize that they are just tape-recorders, not people.

'Similarly, when you are excessively troubled by thoughts, you feel that there are so many thoughts making you unhappy. But when you go within and investigate, you realize that no one is unhappy. We let our thoughts define ourselves, and thus become unhappy. In reality, all thoughts originate from the source—i.e. supreme silence.

'Every person spins a web according to his own beliefs and then grumbles, 'Why is such and such a thing happening? It shouldn't! Why did god create this world? How nice it would have been had he not done so!' In this way, he keeps feeling miserable even though nature has not created any misery. Man forgets his true self in misery and gets lost in his web of thoughts. This so-called misery exists only so that we can understand the true source and attain true happiness. The world has been created for happiness. But man forgets real happiness and gives undue importance to external pleasures. The sympathy offered by others becomes important to him. The true happiness that he was supposed to arrive at through the unhappy event is lost.

'When an inward-bound truth-seeker gets unhappy thoughts, he contemplates upon them and finds such answers that, henceforth, unhappiness doesn't accompany those thoughts even if they rise again. When an average person suffers he says, 'Why do I always have to suffer? Who is responsible for this?' He immediately tries to find a scapegoat to escape his responsibility and obtain relief. He believes that when certain people and circumstances change, only then will he be happy.'

A youngster took the investigation further. 'What must we do to live our life like a seeker? Please guide us.'

Hercules was happy to answer him. He explained, 'A truth-seeker immediately contemplates upon the things that make him suffer, writes them down and eliminates the feeling of unhappiness. He investigates to such an extent that only a feeling of truth remains. If thoughts of untruth such as hatred, guilt, jealousy, etc. do not create any feeling in a person, wouldn't his life be beautiful?

'From morning to night, man harbours some thoughts of truth and some of untruth. The thoughts of truth produce happiness, while thoughts of untruth generate an unpleasant feeling. We should consider the thoughts of untruth to be clouds flitting across the sky. In other words, these thoughts should not make any difference to you. If you can stay happy and unshaken despite those thoughts, then you are on the right track. When you look at unpleasant thoughts through eyes of wisdom, they lose their power. Thoughts of lust and luxury lose their effectiveness when seen through eyes of wisdom.

'Whatever beliefs have taken root inside you, conduct a written investigation about them. Conduct a self-retreat, i.e. contemplate upon them throughout the day. Conduct such a self-retreat at least on your birthday. When you reflect upon each of your beliefs, your negative thoughts will lose power. If your belief is that people don't love you, write down this thought and meditate upon it, in writing, from all angles. After your exploration, you will realize that you do not love yourself. If you loved yourself, would you have worried and tormented yourself about others not loving you? Would you have eaten more than you required and spoiled your body? Would you have let your life be ruined by one wrong belief? Would you have carried this untruth wherever you went? If you had loved yourself, you wouldn't have done any of this.'

The hall reverberated with applause from the audience.

Hercules smiled and said, 'A person who loves himself does not wear tattered clothes because he doesn't want people to laugh at him. Likewise, check if your thoughts are tattered. If you truly love yourself, you will not harbour tattered thoughts, i.e. thoughts that cause you suffering. You don't have to take love—you have to give it, because you have a never-ending, unlimited source of love inside you. What will you do with so much love? Just keep sharing it throughout your life!'

A glum lady said, 'I keep thinking that if my mother had loved me or if my teacher had paid enough attention to me, I would have been something else today.'

Hercules said, 'By thinking in this manner, you are living in the past. You don't even know what mistake you are committing. When you contemplate, the secret will be revealed to you: "There is no sense in what I've been thinking all these years. Why should they love me? Am I a beggar? Do I not have anything? And why do I need love?" Remember, I said that you have the very source of love inside you! Dig deep and ask yourself such questions. Otherwise, the same record will keep playing all your life. Parents live in their children's minds in this manner, even after they die. Now let them carry on with their journey, and you pay attention to yours. Liberate them by saying, "You are free and so am I." There is no reason to tie anyone down.'

Everyone was shaken by this hard-hitting truth. They understood their mistakes and fell into deep thought. Hercules asked them to pen down their self-exploration in a diary. He explained the importance of writing a daily diary, saying, 'Don't be careless about writing in your diary. All sufferings and problems live in the head. Therefore it is essential to offload them, from the head to the diary. Journal writing is an excellent habit for self-development. Decide what you need to do for your development, determine to overcome all the obstacles in your path, and note all this down in your diary.'

At the end of the day, people left the hall in a contemplative mood. Charusheela too had become introspective after listening to Hercules. Filled with deep respect, she left him at the guest house.

At night, Charusheela wished that the workshop could last longer. If it did, people would learn many new things.

The next day at the temple, Hercules was scheduled to speak upon a vital subject: exercise for thoughts.

He began by saying, 'We do yoga and breathing exercises for our body, but no one pays attention to exercise for thoughts. Just as breath goes in and out automatically, similarly thoughts come and go automatically. Whatever happens automatically, we don't bother about or work on. Therefore, we have never asked our thoughts, "Why are you here?" We have never meditated on our thoughts. Our mind keeps racing here and there like a horse without reins. Whatever our thoughts say, we take it to be the gospel truth. This is known as stamping.

'In the exercise for thoughts, thoughts are asked to do a headstand. You might wonder what purpose a headstand would serve thoughts and what kind of health would be achieved by turning thoughts upside down. The fact is that you can attain equanimity and a balanced state of mind only by exercising your thoughts. This state cannot be achieved without stopping the constant chatter of the mind. Until now, you have hardly ever exercised your thoughts. Only when you have to earn money, make some assets for your house or invent something do you exercise your thoughts. But you never pay any attention to the fact that exercise for thoughts can help you get rid of suffering. The moment man considers his body to be his self, he considers the thoughts arising in the body to be true. He thinks that, since this thought has arisen in his body, it must be right. But the truth is that you can be happy only when you let go of the feeling of always being right, which is the ego. The ego says, 'Whatever thought appears in my body is the right thought.'

But if you have the knowledge of truth, you will not consider only your body to be your self. Then your belief that only those thoughts which arise in your body are true will break. After that, you will not put labels of right or wrong on thoughts and your real investigation will begin. At that time, you must give importance to the truth and not think of who gets the credit.

'It is important to understand what the thoughts are trying to convey. Whenever a thought arises in your mind, it not only informs you about the witness of those thoughts—the Self—but also provides some clues, such as: what belief am I stuck on? What is my need at the moment? Once you start investigating your thoughts, you understand that other people are mirrors asking you to put on your makeup or, in other words, asking you to introspect and change. So, are you putting on your makeup or not? You will change only when you apply your makeup. The mirror tells the truth about others but doesn't know anything about itself. Man too is busy in understanding everything else but himself. You have been applying makeup on others for all these years and you have seen the results.

In trying to improve others, you made no improvements in yourself. Or even if you did change a little, that change didn't last long. You live in the illusion that everything is going fine. But a little something happens and you get upset and create a furore. When you apply makeup on each thought, then you will know that you've got the right end of the thread which will untangle the mess.'

Hercules concluded his talk and asked the audience, 'If anyone has any questions or concerns, you may ask me now.'

A girl in the front row said, 'My thoughts always leave me totally confused. This causes me suffering. What mental exercise should I do to cure this problem?'

'Confusion means having two different thoughts on one subject,' said Hercules. 'As long as you harbour contradictory thoughts about an issue you will stay in confusion. The suffering tells you to decide on one thought. Whenever you feel confused, write your thoughts down and deliberate upon them. Tell yourself, 'I will contemplate on this until I get a shifting—a Eureka moment.'

'When you go to meet confusion, don't go alone. Take your understanding with you. If you go alone, your confusion will be compounded. Life wishes to open you up completely in all circumstances. You must stay present in each experience. This will take care of your confusion.'

Another lady said, 'I'm troubled by all kinds of thoughts throughout the day. What should I do?'

'This is natural,' Hercules replied. 'Do not impose the condition that you should never get thoughts. Thoughts come and go so that your mind stays well-oiled and you remain aware. Thoughts keep occurring to you so that, when the time for inner investigation comes, you can think well and find an immediate solution. When you observe people around you, thoughts related to them will appear—that's not a problem. If you dream that you are looking for a job, will you get up in the morning and be troubled by it?'

'No. I'll say that it was just a dream and that there's no need to be bothered by it.'

'You have to look at your thoughts in the same way. Thoughts pass by, the way clouds do.'

'Thank you,' the woman said.

A man presented his problem saying, 'My mind is always crammed with thoughts. I am very troubled by this. I don't know how to get rid of them. The doctor says that my hypertension is not getting better because I'm thinking too much.'

Hercules said, 'Suppose your mirror has a design on it. Will you get troubled by it every time you look at the mirror? No, because you know that the design makes no difference to you. Similarly, the reality is that your body is your mirror and the thoughts arising in it are like the design on the mirror. As long as the body is doing its job, where is the need to complain? You can complain if the body stops working as a mirror. But the body never falters in its role. Even when lying in a hospital, it continues to work as a mirror!

'This investigation will stop your fight with unwanted thoughts and remove your resistance towards them. Even then, if your mind runs after thoughts, just say, "That's okay. Now that I remember, let's return to the Source or the centre." Ask yourself, "I'm getting some thoughts, but where are they exactly?" When you ask yourself, you will know that nothing is happening to you—it is happening for you. In other words, thoughts are occurring on a mirror or a screen in front of you. You can see the thoughts, which means that you possess awareness. When you look at a scene, you get proof that you have eyes. Similarly, when thoughts appear, they give you proof that you are there. You are separate from your thoughts because the knower of thoughts is not a thought. Just like the one seeing a scene is not the scene, and the one smelling a fragrance is not the fragrance. Who is the one experiencing or knowing all these things? When you come to know the answer, your resistance towards thoughts will fade away.'

'Yes, at some level I did have this belief that having so many thoughts is not right. Now this belief is changing. I've come to realize that thoughts are not me. I'm the knower of those thoughts,' said the man.

'Brilliant! Actually, man is unable to use his intellect to the fullest. You can see a lot of things in the sky from morning till night. Sometimes when the sky is empty, you consider it normal. Clouds keep floating by but they don't bother you. Similarly, thoughts keep floating across your mind. Take advantage of them instead of letting them become an obstacle. Just give a direction to your thoughts and lay back. Tell your thoughts, "All right, tell me about what I'm experiencing. If you want to say something, tell me who I am." Then your thoughts will start moving in that direction and become your servant. When you don't use them, they go to waste.'

'Please guide us further on how to make our thoughts our servant,' another participant said.

'If you don't give work to your servant, what will he do?' said Hercules. 'He will keep transferring grain from one container to another and create problems for you. He will move everything from one place to another. Then you will keep looking for them. You must not keep him idle. You must give him something to do. Likewise, give the right direction to your thoughts, otherwise they will keep running here and there and trouble you. Breath comes and goes on its own, but you are not troubled by it. Thoughts too come and go automatically, but you are troubled by them because you believe that you are doing the thinking. When you will think of who you are in reality, then there is no problem. Thoughts have been created so that we can think about our true self. But until we think about our true self, what will the mind do? A machine should keep functioning, otherwise it becomes rusty. If the machine of your body doesn't have any thoughts, and one day you wish to think about your true self, you will find that the machine is not working. If thoughts keep arising every day, know that your machine is working properly. If the machine keeps functioning, it will stay healthy. If it shuts down, then it won't work when you need it to. You will need a mechanic to set it right. You will need to oil it. It's good that it functions automatically—you don't have to make any effort to operate it. It is functioning so that one day, it can help you in knowing your true self. Why fight with such a machine? Just understand your responsibility, that's all!'

'Oh! I didn't know that this was the purpose of my body and my thoughts!' exclaimed the participant.

Lastly, a software engineer asked, 'One thought always keeps bothering me—in my profession, I need to learn new things and update myself every day. I find that difficult. I am unable to assimilate change. How do I investigate this thought?'

Hercules replied, '"I am unable to assimilate change." This thought is the obstacle in your progress. If you change this thought you will overcome your problem. This thought means that you are convinced, "I can do only this much. This is my capacity. This is my limitation. I can't do anything more." That's not true. You can do a lot more. Your capability is much more than what you think it is. By thinking that you are not handsome or that you have low self-confidence or that you don't have contacts or money, etc. you limit your self-expression. If the power of thought is awakened, even tasks which seem impossible can be accomplished.

'Once a person in a gym was asked how much weight he could lift and he said 30 kg. He was then hypnotized and given certain instructions. In that state of hypnosis, he could lift 50 kg. All this was recorded on video and, when it was shown to him subsequently, his self-confidence escalated to a whole new level. The limitation of his thought was shattered. Man's thoughts have many limitations. He should keep performing small experiments to go beyond these limitations. After each experiment, his self-confidence will increase.'

As always, Hercules was carrying some copies of *The Path to Peace*. He handed them over to the temple organizers. Since the number of participants was very large, he requested the organizers to procure more copies and distribute them.

For the next couple of days, the evening talks by Hercules continued. Hercules participated in all the programmes that Parimal had lined up for him and, thereafter, left for India. Parimal bade him goodbye with great reverence.

As the aeroplane took off, contemplation took off inside Hercules' mind. He realized that the workshop and the talks had been a medium for his own exploration of thought. He was astounded at the words that came out of his mouth during the workshop and the talks. He was ecstatic and grateful. Earlier, he used to identify with his thoughts and therefore, be troubled by them. He never looked at them from a higher plane. He understood that if he had taken a bird's eye view, he would never have had to suffer from anything. He suddenly remembered the dark night when he had run over a woman because he had been drowning in the whirlpool of his thoughts. He'd had to flee like a pitiful criminal. It was the Goddess' grace that he was here today. Now, through self-exploration, he was attaining freedom from all his suffering and beliefs. He realized that he'd not even had a migraine in the past two months. He had totally forgotten about it. This is when he suddenly experienced his Eureka moment. He realized that all this while, he himself had been inviting the migraine by keeping the memory of it alive! Now that he had flushed it out of his mind, he was sure that it would not return.

It was the full-moon night when Hercules arrived at the temple. In the days that Hercules had been away, the priest had reflected in depth and come to realize that he had unnecessarily fallen into the trap of guilt. He recalled how people confessed their wrong deeds to Hercules and, saying that committing mistakes was natural, Hercules provided them solutions. Having seen this, he felt the burden lift from his head. He decided that he too would confess everything to

Hercules. He felt lighter after making this decision. A desire for pure conduct had awakened in him and he was impatiently waiting for Hercules.

As soon as Hercules reached the temple, the priest embraced him. Hercules was pleasantly surprised. He freshened up, had some food and came and sat with the priest on the steps of the temple. He started talking about his experiences during the journey. And, for the first time, the priest was listening to and conversing with Hercules with an open mind and real joy. All around them, the full moon was spreading its soothing, tranquil light. The temple was decorated with arcs of light. The compound was beautifully lit with arrays of oil-lamps. People had left the temple, but the priest continued to talk to Hercules.

Hercules was amazed by this change in the priest's behaviour. He forgot his tiredness and exchanged thoughts with the priest late into the night. Sometimes they would both get lost in their respective thoughts and drift into silence. Then, a thought would start their conversation once more. Both were praising each other. Their respect for each other was growing. They were so engrossed in their contemplation and exchange of thoughts that they didn't realize when dawn broke. On one side, the full moon was setting, and on the other, the sun was rising. They gazed at this magnificent sight for a long time. Both of them experienced the same feeling—the setting of negative feelings, beliefs and suffering, and the rise of positive feelings, joy and truth… total bliss.

Seven

The Sixth Task of Hercules: Reigning the Mares —Investigating False Beliefs

The priest handed a letter to a surprised Hercules who read it after his morning prayers. In the letter, the priest had confessed all his wrongdoings and poured his heart out. He had written all about his beliefs, stampings, thoughts, good and bad qualities, fears and insecurities without holding back anything. He had written everything about his drug trafficking and how he had given it up. Hercules read the letter and was shocked. However, he also felt very happy about the priest's change of heart. For him, the priest's mind becoming peaceful, pure and loving was nothing less than a reward. 'He is the ninth!' a voice inside him said. Hercules was overjoyed. His penance was now bearing fruit.

The priest was feeling cleansed and liberated after confessing everything to Hercules, as though all the poison had been drained out from his heart. For the first time he was experiencing purity. In this blissful state, some new thoughts entered his mind and he smiled. As he entered the temple, Hercules looked at him and asked, 'What are you smiling at?'

'Nothing!'

'Oh! The mind is happy because of nothingness, isn't it?'

'Exactly. That's how it is.'

No one spoke about the letter but both understood what this exchange meant.

'Thanks to divine grace, I'm achieving success in my mission. Now I eagerly await your next instruction,' said Hercules, changing the topic.

'I shall end your wait right here. After you left for Mauritius, the gentleman who had written to me earlier came to ask for my daughter's hand in marriage for his son. Our talks were successful. The wedding is scheduled in fifteen days and your presence is important. This is my next task for you.'

Hercules was confounded by this unusual task. He agreed to attend the wedding thinking, 'There must be some hidden boon in this as well.'

The priest handed over the responsibility of the temple to a long-time devotee and left for his village along with Hercules. On reaching home, the priest introduced Hercules to his family: his wife Rukmini, his daughter, his younger brother Lakhan and Lakhan's wife Urmila. He also told them about Hercules' wisdom and teachings. After a few days, Maya and Mahesh also arrived. They were thrilled to meet Hercules once again.

At last, the wait was over. The groom's party arrived one day before the wedding. Religious rituals and cultural programmes began in the evening. The atmosphere was pleasant and cheerful. The priest left no stone unturned in hosting the groom's party. He ensured that all their needs were fulfilled and that they were comfortable. But on the day of the wedding, Hercules noticed some discordant voices during the rituals. The priest and Rukmini showed signs of anxiety. People started whispering to each other. The priest somehow managed the situation and solemnized the marriage. The groom's party departed after the ceremony without any further hitch.

The priest was busy with the accounts for the next couple of days and Hercules assisted him in every possible way. Most of the relatives left for their homes. Now only the priest, Rukmini, Lakhan, Urmila, Mahesh, Maya and Hercules were left. They sat in the veranda and started discussing the wedding.

Rukmini was sad and discontented. Not only had their daughter departed to her in-laws' home, but the groom's party had created unpleasantness as well.

Urmila spoke in a low tone, 'What the groom's party did was not good. We did everything we could but that didn't stop them from finding fault with our arrangements.'

'Such things happen during weddings. Why are you taking it to heart?' Lakhan tried to reason with her.

Hearing this, Rukmini lost her cool. 'What are you saying? The other party behaves any which way and you justify their behaviour by saying such things happen? That's not fair. I have never seen such rude people.'

'What happened?' Hercules asked, sensing the seriousness of the situation.

'There was some unpleasantness regarding the dowry, their lodging arrangements and a slight difference in wedding rituals. All this led to a tense situation and some argument. That's why everyone is upset,' Lakhan told him.

Hercules tried to console them and said, 'Will you please tell me, one by one, your reasons for being upset?'

Rukmini was filled with rancour. She immediately started venting her anger. She said, 'During the wedding rituals, our priest and the groom's priest did not agree upon some rituals. We had procured all the things required for the ceremony as directed by our priest, but the groom's priest found it inadequate. He said, "Such ignorance in a priest's family!" He insulted us by calling us ignorant. Even the groom's father sided with their priest. I had such wonderful expectations from the marriage—a loving relationship with my daughter's in-laws, fun-filled moments… but all that was not to be.'

Urmila said, 'We gave them exquisite jewellery and expensive clothes as dowry, but they were not satisfied. Isn't that wrong? I wonder what they think of themselves. I feel they had come here determined to harass us.'

The priest said, 'All of them were rather indolent. They didn't value time. I didn't like their laziness.'

Maya said, 'They had told us to expect a certain number of guests but many more turned up and it became difficult to arrange for their stay at the last minute.'

Thus, everyone had some complaint or the other. Hercules listened attentively to all of them.

Suddenly, the priest remembered *The Path to Peace*. He asked everyone to be quiet and told them about Hercules' inner investigation therapy. 'Do you want freedom from the suffering that has originated from your complaints?' he asked.

Everyone replied in the affirmative.

'All right, then. We will hear Hercules' wise words every day. Are you ready?'

This proposal pleased Mahesh and Maya the most. Rukmini and

Urmila exchanged glances as if to say, 'I wonder who he is. We may get bored. We already know about the ways of the world—what will he teach us?' But they didn't have the courage to say no to the head of the family. Lakhan too was in the same situation. They all agreed, albeit reluctantly. A unanimous decision was taken to gather every evening.

The meeting was dispersed and people returned to their respective chores. Only Hercules and the priest remained in the veranda. The priest requested Hercules to extend his stay in order to provide guidance to his family. Hercules readily agreed.

At seven in the evening, the family gathered in the veranda. Hercules greeted everyone and said, 'All of you have gathered here with a very noble aim. Very few people develop a desire to stay happy under all circumstances. Therefore, I welcome you all. From today onwards, I shall tell you truths that will help you achieve your aim of happiness—provided you incorporate these truths in your daily lives.

'In an individual's life, happy and unhappy events occur all the time. Man has come to earth in order to learn the art of remaining unshaken under all circumstances. He can help himself and others only if he remains unshaken, otherwise he makes the situation more difficult. Today, all of you are unhappy because of some disturbances during the wedding. But if you dig deep within and investigate, you can come out of this situation. All the actual causes of your unhappiness can be brought to light.'

'We know that our sufferings are caused either by people or by circumstances. What is there to investigate?' asked Rukmini.

'You have to investigate within yourself and your nature. You have to examine what makes you sad and what makes you happy. But man always considers himself to be right and blames people or circumstances for his unhappiness. Here is where he puts a full stop to the investigation because of his inner beliefs and made-up stories. Therefore, it is essential to keep your beliefs aside and begin your investigation.'

Hercules' words were like a recap for the priest, Mahesh and Maya. But the others were struggling to understand the import of his words. Hercules carried on, 'Very often, man's ego comes in the way of his self-investigation. He doesn't wish to unmask himself in front of others. So much so that he keeps his real face hidden from himself as well. That is why some rules have been made for investigation. Tomorrow we shall discuss these rules.'

'Does this mean that our complaints are unjustified?' asked Rukmini in astonishment.

In answer to this question, Hercules gave a copy of *The Path to Peace* to each one of them. He requested them to read the first chapter before the next day's meeting.

Just then, a woman entered calling for Rukmini. She stopped in her tracks when she saw the gathering. Rukmini beckoned to her and said, 'Come Tulsi. You've come at the right time. You too can join us.' Tulsi had lent a hand in the wedding arrangements just like a family member. Rukmini introduced Tulsi to Hercules and said, 'She is our tenant, but we have such good relations with her that we consider her a member of this household. She is a teacher in the local school.'

Hercules greeted Tulsi. They all decided to gather again the next day, at the same time. The women sat chatting while the men dispersed.

Tulsi took *The Path to Peace* from Rukmini's hands and started flipping through its pages. Rukmini apprised Tulsi of all that had transpired in the session with Hercules and invited her to their next gathering.

Urmila said, 'Let's read the first chapter together.'

Tulsi agreed and started reading. After reading they started discussing stamping, labelling, beliefs, made-up stories, etc. Soon it was time to prepare dinner, which they did—all the while, pondering over these concepts.

The next day, they all gathered at the appointed time. Surprisingly, everyone had done their homework. Rukmini whispered into Urmila's ears, 'We were wrong. I think there is some substance to Hercules' words and his book. I liked it.' Urmila nodded in agreement. Just then, Hercules made his entry. Lakhan smiled and said, 'The first chapter has prepared us to listen, to some extent. Therefore, please begin with today's discourse.'

Hercules smiled and began, 'It is important to follow some rules while performing inner investigation. The first rule is that you must speak with yourself honestly and without any deception, and recognize your beliefs, such as: "That person didn't listen to me, I felt bad," or "I was humiliated in front of others, I felt bad," or "If only it had happened differently, it would've been so much better." Take into consideration all such thoughts that arose during the wedding.'

'We mentioned some of those yesterday,' said Urmila.

'Yes, but now you all have to investigate them. If these thoughts are making you unhappy, do you want to remain unhappy all your life?' asked Hercules.

'Not at all!'

'Then you will need to change your thinking. You will need to look at your thoughts from different perspectives. Things didn't happen the way you wanted them to, that is why you are doing this investigation. If everything had happened according to your expectations, would we be gathering here? Would you have begun your investigation?'

'Right. At least we've all gotten ready for this investigation,' everybody agreed.

Hercules began to explain the concept of self-investigation. 'If someone calls you lazy, you don't believe him because you consider yourself to be a responsible person. You say, "I get up early in the morning and go for a morning walk. I work honestly throughout the day." You present various arguments against your alleged laziness. But there are many things that others can do but you cannot. Aren't you shirking work when it comes to those particular tasks? Not only that, you also invent innumerable excuses for not doing them.'

'Now I am able to understand a little,' said Rukmini. And after thinking for a while, she added, 'When the groom's priest called us ignorant, I found it very insulting. How could he call us ignorant? I am the one who carries out all religious rituals with great responsibility. On top of that, my husband is a temple priest! And their priest was trying to educate us? But now, after listening to you, I feel compelled to look at the areas where I am actually ignorant.'

Hercules said, 'Yes, this is the right way to investigate within. One person finds something very easy while another finds it difficult. Some people can easily get up early in the morning. They immediately label late-risers as lazy and irresponsible. Some people get up late but that doesn't make them lazy. Therefore, do not label people.

If you keep finding faults with people, your good habits too will make you unhappy. And if a good habit is causing you unhappiness, then how can it be good? Stop trying to prove that you are right. Look into all areas of your life and find the ones where you are indulging in exactly the same thing that you are complaining about.

If someone calls you lazy, stop becoming unhappy. Just get your act together and investigate all the areas in which you are being lazy, in every sphere of life.'

Rukmini responded at once, 'Now I understand. I may be an expert in household chores and religious rituals, but I am ignorant about many other things like doing bank work, paying the electricity and telephone bills, using mobile phones and computers, and so on.'

The priest said, 'I'm very punctual and get upset with people who don't understand the value of time. According to you, is the good habit of being punctual a cause of my suffering?'

'Yes, definitely. Let us understand this through an example,' said Hercules. 'A man feeds grain to the crows every morning and thinks that this is a very good habit. But this habit becomes the cause of his suffering. He notices the crows fighting over the grain and feels unhappy. So you see, his good habit of feeding the crows becomes a cause for unhappiness. If the crows fight, you need not feel unhappy. You have done good work. That is all. What the others do about it is not your concern. Otherwise your good habit will become the cause of your unhappiness.'

'I get it! I have been getting unnecessarily worked up about the fact that people are not as punctual as I am,' said the priest.

'We feel like laughing at our foolishness,' everyone said in unison.

Tulsi said, 'How easily we are able to laugh at our foolishness in front of Hercules. Could we have done this in front of anyone else? This is surprising!'

'This is the magic of truth. Falsehood disappears in the presence of truth,' said Hercules. 'Now, let's return to our subject. You need to investigate the cause of your suffering and look for its solution by being truthful to yourself. Always remember the first rule of self-investigation: speak to yourself with complete honesty. Your work should start with this rule. Stop covering your vices with the garb of your virtues. A person who is deceitful with himself can never progress in life. Be completely honest with yourself and ask, "Do I feel bad if my neighbour buys a new car?" If the answer is yes, then search for the belief imprinted inside you which is the cause of your suffering. Your exploration will bring your belief to light. You can then work upon your belief and become free forever. Therefore, stop deceiving yourself this very moment.

'In a mental asylum, a patient was playing cards with himself. A visitor was observing him play. He asked the patient, "What's this! Why are you cheating yourself?" The patient said, "Speak softly. I've been doing this for the past ten years." The visitor asked, "You've been cheating yourself for ten years? Didn't you ever catch yourself?" The patient replied, "I'm very smart. I don't let myself get caught." That man is unaware of his own foolishness. He is the smartest as well as the most foolish because he doesn't know that he is causing great harm to himself by this self-deception.

'You also cheat yourself and consider yourself smart. You make yourself suffer and hide this fact from yourself by trying to prove that someone else is making you suffer. If you wish to stop suffering, let go of this foolishness and be honest with yourself. Your actual investigation will begin only after you apprise yourself of this reality. During your investigation you might not find the answers immediately, but continue investigating. One day your investigation will surely reach completion.'

Everyone expressed their gratitude to Hercules and promised to return the next day only after speaking honestly with themselves. All the men got busy with their work, and the women decided that, instead of entertaining unnecessary thoughts, they would speak honestly with themselves while working in the kitchen.

The next day, everyone gathered in the veranda. They were eager to share the honest conversations they'd had with themselves.

Rukmini said, 'I am the eldest woman in this house. I also happen to be the eldest of my siblings. I know how to shoulder my responsibilities. I feel proud of this fact. But this quality gradually made me egoistic. I consider others to be inferior to me. This belief is the basis of all my thoughts and actions. As a result, sometimes people get hurt and react in a manner that hurts me. Thus, we keep hurting each other, stuck in a vicious cycle of our own making.'

Urmila looked at her sister-in-law with wonder. She felt that Rukmini had managed to catch the pulse of their relationship. She said, 'My contemplation made me realize that each person evaluates everything based on his own beliefs. He decides the quality of a thing according to his own beliefs. It is possible that the groom's side honestly didn't like the clothes and ornaments, but we made up the story that it was their sole intention to harass us. We keep spinning these tales one after another and as a result of this, our suffering never ends.'

'Very good. Please keep conversing with yourself with such honesty.'

'We wish to know the second rule of investigation today,' Lakhan said.

'Certainly! The second rule of investigation says: give importance to your self-experience. For example, the calendar tells you your age, but do not trust it. The clock tells you that you have worked for so many hours, but do not trust it. You get up in the morning, look at your watch and say, "Oh, I slept for just five hours," and feel weary. But if somebody, while you slept, had advanced the watch by two hours, you would have remarked, "Wow! I slept very well today."

This means that you do not give importance to your own experience. You give importance to the time shown by the clock, the date seen on the calendar, the opinions expressed by others, and so on.

'Pay attention to what your self-experience tells you about your complaints. Did you feel bad when the event happened, or are you feeling bad only now? Say someone slapped you ten years ago. You felt pain at that time which is understandable, but you are feeling that pain even now. Isn't that too much? Just think—is someone really slapping you today or are you making yourself unhappy just by thinking about an event that happened ten years ago? On investigation, you will know that your repeated thoughts about that incident are making you suffer. Otherwise, the pain went away a long time ago. So, the second rule of investigation is: tell yourself the truth based on your self-experience.

'Let's take up an anecdote for more clarity. Three people got together and were going somewhere. One of them was a barber, one was a bald man and one was a fool. They carried on with their journey until it was dark and then stopped for some sleep. They decided to take turns standing guard for three hours at a time, while the other two slept.

'First, the bald man and the fool went to sleep while the barber stood guard. The barber thought, "How should I pass these three hours? Let me do what I do best—cut hair." Since there was no question of cutting the bald man's hair, he started cutting the foolish man's hair. His time passed happily, while he did the work he loved. Eventually, not a hair was left on the foolish man's head. After three hours, the barber woke the fool up and said, "Now it's your turn to stand guard. I'm going to sleep." The fool got up, stretched, scratched his head and went back to sleep saying, "You've woken up the bald man by mistake."'

Everybody burst into laughter.

Hercules continued, 'You always think that the other person is making a mistake, but it is possible that you are making a mistake. The fool thinks that the barber is mistaken, but the reality is that he is mistaken. His self-experience tells him that he has woken up but he doesn't pay attention to it. He touches his bald head and thinks that the barber has woken up the bald man. In other words, man ignores his self-experience and gets stuck in illusory truths. Therefore, pay attention to your self-experience while investigating. Along with this, you should understand that whatever is happening is happening for you, not to you. It is happening to give you happiness. This is the truth. Are you deriving happiness? Are you giving importance to your self-experience? If not, then you are committing a mistake by getting trapped in your beliefs and stories.'

Everyone was swept away by Hercules' subtle analysis. They realized that very often they took decisions keeping the situation and people in mind. They never focussed on their self-experience. Rukmini said, 'Some or the other belief is always influencing our every action. We weigh every action on the scale of right or wrong.'

'Just understand that all these follies keep recurring because you are not focussed on your self-experience,' Hercules said. 'Therefore, I request all of you to conduct some inner investigation and find out all those areas where you don't pay attention to your self-experience. We shall meet again tomorrow.'

The next day, everyone came before time and sat in quiet contemplation. The priest broke the silence saying, 'Now I am beginning to understand how we overlook self-experience because we are stuck in our beliefs.'

'Can you explain that?' Hercules asked.

'Sure. I feel fresh even after sleeping for just five hours, but I have read in various books and articles that one must sleep for eight hours a day in order to remain healthy. Hence, I feel that I have not slept well. In this way, I ignore my self-experience and get entangled in bookish knowledge,' said the priest.

Tulsi said, 'I too have formed a limit for my capacity to work. I can easily spend an entire day evaluating answer-sheets during the annual exams without feeling tired at all. But when my colleagues complain about feeling tired, I start nodding in agreement and start feeling tired myself. I ignore my self-experience and get influenced by others. Perhaps we trust people's views more than we trust our own experience.'

Hercules concurred and said, 'What you feel is not always true. When it's clear to you that there are some other things hidden behind your suffering, you will be able to investigate your self with love and happiness. Your source wants you to be happy all the time. When you are happy, you are with your source, you are with your self-experience. But when you are unhappy, you are with your beliefs. Whenever your mind says, "I feel like this, I feel like that," do not believe it at once. Whatever the mind may say, do not stamp on it. Just begin your investigation. You will find the truth only through investigation. Otherwise, by blindly trusting the stories of your mind, you will suffer all your life.

'For example: a person had several physical flaws. His nose was unusually big, his mouth was aslant, his ears were big and his hair was coarse. He was employed in an average job. He used to feel, "I have so many physical and economical shortcomings that people must think of me as an inferior fellow. If I go to a shop to purchase something, the shopkeeper will ignore me. Not only that, even my friends are not fond of my company." He was always sad due to these made-up stories. One day, he asked one of his friends, "What do you feel when you look at me?" The friend replied, "I feel good when I look at you. I feel very happy." This answer surprised him. He said, "I used to feel that you think badly of me and consider me your inferior." Now it was his friend's turn to be astonished. He asked, "Why? Why would you feel that way?" The man replied, "Because of my face and my job." The friend exclaimed, "Not at all! If I had known that you are so sensitive about your face and job, I would have clarified this earlier—I like you very much." This example tells you that when that person did some investigation, he came to know that he was unhappy just because he felt some things. There was no need at all for him to suffer so much.'

Urmila was slightly less good-looking than the rest of the family, therefore she always felt inferior to the others. Now she wondered if this unhappiness was a result of her perception alone.

Hercules carried on. 'Some social beliefs were created around people's physical deformities so as to protect them from ridicule. For example, someone with six fingers is considered to be lucky. Otherwise, people make fun of those with physical defects. In schools and colleges such youngsters are labelled as inferior to the others. The fact is that six fingers do not make one lucky or unlucky. Actually, nothing in this world has a label on it but we are not able to understand things without labelling them, hence they are labelled: camera, speaker, table, watch, book, etc. Labels that don't make us unhappy are fine, but we need to do something about the labels that trouble us.

'Just look at it this way. If we were to number each item in this world—for example, number 1 for camera, number 2 for book, number 3 for table, and so on—what would happen? You wouldn't call a tree a tree, but call it number 115. Similarly, if people were given numbers, no one would say, "He is dark," or, "He is fair." If the dark person was given the number 36 and the fair person was 46, would anyone feel bad or sad?'

'That's a great idea!' Lakhan said.

Tulsi liked the idea too, but she had another problem and wanted its solution. She said, 'I am often troubled by thoughts like, "If only it was like this. If only it was like that. If only this had not happened." And so on. Is there a hidden belief behind all of this?'

'Of course! The belief behind this way of thinking is that whatever is happening with you is not good, while whatever is not happening with you is good. But please understand that wishes are like a vessel without a base—it can never fill up. Whatever is happening with you in the present is the reality. What you are thinking about is not. If you live in a world of regret, it means you love only your make-believe stories. Whatever you have today, accept it and love it. When you think, "I wish this had happened. How wonderful it would have been," it indicates that you need self-investigation.'

'Today you have told us the bitter truth of life. Our beliefs and stories are the main cause of our suffering,' said Mahesh.

Hercules replied, 'When you stop loving your make-believe stories and stop labelling others, you will begin to see everything clearly. Then you will know that thoughts start when you stop seeing. Leave these beliefs and start investigating. Ask yourself whether whatever is happening in your life is making you see yourself.'

Everyone understood the meaning of beliefs and make-believe stories in the true sense.

The priest said, 'I have been listening to you for so many days, but today I have actually understood how we invite events into our lives because of our beliefs. I am convinced that this is the root cause of our suffering.'

Maya said, 'We shall try to identify our beliefs through contemplation and share it at the meeting tomorrow.'

The meeting ended and everyone got up and went about their daily routine. All the while, they kept mulling over the various beliefs that were trapping them.

The next day, they all gathered in a celebratory mood. Their faces reflected their encounter with their beliefs.

Urmila started with her story first. 'Yesterday I investigated deeply into my beliefs. I was born and brought up in this village. All my education took place here and I also got married here. I have no clue about urban life and its ways. Some of our relatives live in cities. I feel inferior to them. This inferiority complex has been in my mind since childhood. When I explored the beliefs behind this suffering, I found a new respect for myself.'

Hercules said, 'Superb! When you love and respect yourself, only then will you receive love and respect from others. But remember that you are loving and respecting yourself because you understand the truth and not because you want love and respect from others. The torch of understanding should stay ablaze throughout your life and not get extinguished.'

Lakhan spoke next. 'I too wish to share one of my beliefs. Since I'm from a Brahmin family and conduct prayers and rituals at people's homes, I regard myself to be superior to other castes. This belief of mine has given rise to an attitude of discrimination. I do not even drink water in lower caste homes. Today I wonder if this is a false belief.'

'Indeed! This is one of man's deepest beliefs,' said Hercules. 'Man receives the label of caste after he is born. In reality, he is nameless and casteless. It is nothing great to be born in a Brahmin family—but it is truly great to die a Brahmin.'

'What does that mean?' asked Lakhan.

'Dying a Brahmin means dissolving into Brahma after the death of the body. It means being able to experience being during death. Only a true Brahmin can do this, even though he may have taken birth in an untouchable's family,' said Hercules.

'We have been living with such a massive delusion all our lives!' Maya gave voice to everyone's thoughts.

Hercules continued, 'Living in truth for just one day is better than living a hundred years with beliefs. The ultimate purpose of your life on earth is to attain the truth. The biggest belief keeping you away from the truth is considering your body to be your Self. The body is just an instrument of your true self. In other words, your body is a doorway to gain entry into this world. Just as a microphone is only an instrument through which we amplify our voice, similarly our body is a mechanism through which our true self speaks. We need to understand who the speaker is. The moment you come to know your true self, i.e. attain self-realization, you will also know that the body is merely a medium for the self to experience and express itself.'

There was pin-drop silence for some time. Ego lost its existence in the light of truth.

After a while, during which everyone tried to comprehend the most profound truth of life, Rukmini asked, 'As I told you, we could not perform some rituals because of some misunderstanding between the two sides. That is why my mind fears that the gods will be angry with us and something unfortunate might happen. Is this also just a belief?'

'Yes, this too is just a belief. The fear of God is completely unnecessary. This fear has been sown in our minds so that everyone in society sticks to doing good. You should perform religious rituals not because you fear god but because you understand, respect and love god. God is love, and love never gets angry.'

Everyone was elated when they heard this.

Lakhan said, 'For the last few days, you have been advising us to stay happy at all times. But there is so much unrest throughout the world. War clouds are always hovering somewhere. No one can say who will attack whom and when. Every nation wants to become a superpower. How can anyone live without fear?'

Hercules replied, 'This fear is related to your belief that there is unrest in the world and hence there is unrest inside us and so we cannot stay happy. If you actually want to stop wars, don't just say it—do it! People say wars can be stopped by doing this or that, but they themselves do nothing. The reality is that if you wish to stop wars, if you want to bring peace and harmony in this world, then you must first stop the war inside you. The moment your internal war ends, that very moment will be the beginning of the end of war in this world.

'When you feel disturbed by the fights amongst your friends and family, just ask yourself, 'Have you stopped the fight taking place inside you? Is your inner war over?' The fact is that by fighting, your friends and family are reminding you to investigate the fights within yourself and to remember the truth. People say that they don't like any conflict at home, but out of ignorance they keep strengthening the conflict inside themselves by feeding it with malicious thoughts. You have to achieve inner peace before you can achieve outer peace. If you investigate, you will realize that you raise fingers at others. You say so-and-so is scared of rats and you ridicule him. But it never occurs to you that even you are scared of some things—of conflicts for instance. When you investigate in this manner, you will start appreciating the answers that seem contradictory.

'Therefore, please do what you have come to do on this earth. Do not fear unrest and try to make your mind steadfast. When we complain about unrest, we move away from ourselves. Use whatever opportunities you get to look within. Could you have done all this homework by yourself? Could you have remembered all these things? That is why people and events come to remind you about your purpose. They keep showing you a mirror. This is the world's most beautiful arrangement. Take full advantage of it.'

Everyone's face lit up with feelings of gratitude, but Tulsi was still in some confusion. Hercules asked, 'Do you have any doubts left?'

Tulsi said, 'One thing has been bothering me for a long time. I met with an accident about a year ago. I was going on my scooter when suddenly a speeding motorcycle hit me and raced off. I fell down and was badly hurt. One of my legs had compound fractures. I had to be hospitalized for a long time.'

Tulsi's words made Hercules' heart tremble. The dreadful scene of the accident that had occurred last year, on the 12th of December, flashed before his eyes.

'What happened after that?' Urmila was curious.

'I got better, but my leg is still weak. At school I have to stand for long periods to teach in the classes. By evening my leg starts aching terribly. My mind always goes back to that incident. Why me? Why did that accident have to happen to me? Why did god play such a game with me? I am unable to forgive that motorcyclist. I had to suffer so much pain because of him. The memory of that dark night troubles me ever so often. What is the belief behind this misery? I am unable to investigate that. Will you please guide me regarding this?'

Hercules listened to Tulsi and closed his eyes. 'Is she the same person? She is alive? Was I carrying unnecessary guilt all these days?' After a few moments of silence, the light of truth dawned. 'If I had known that the woman was alive, would I have left home with the intense feeling of repentance? Would I have discovered the life-transforming tool of inner investigation? Would I have achieved freedom from my tendencies? Would I have become a medium of empowerment for others? No! Ignorance of the fact that the woman was alive proved to be very beneficial for me.'

Tulsi waited for Hercules to answer her, but when he didn't she repeated her question. Her words pulled Hercules out from his trance. He asked haltingly, 'Where did this accident take place?'

'It occurred in my ancestral town of Sonbaag last year, on the 12th of December, on the highway. I used to teach in a school there. I was under treatment for four months after the accident and then I was transferred here.'

This information confirmed Hercules' doubt. He thought, 'Tulsi has been instrumental in my penance!' His heart was filled with amazement, joy, gratitude and many other emotions. He thought, 'Oh god! I lived with this guilt needlessly for so many days. You have solved a major problem of my life.'

He controlled his emotions and told Tulsi, 'Whatever happened to you, just understand that it is what you needed. Whenever anything happens to you, make full use of it. Each event is telling you something about yourself. From morning till night, even in your dreams, you are being told something but you do not listen to it. You only listen to what your belief says. Like you said, you had to undergo a lot of physical suffering because of your accident. This incident is also telling you something. But you label it as bad and do not listen to what it is trying to tell to you.'

'I don't understand. How can I need an accident?' asked Tulsi.

'Please contemplate on all the good things that have happened in your life after that incident—what are the things that you have started doing because of the accident and wouldn't have done otherwise? Then you will understand that an accident also has its own role. It comes to make us do something. Now let us consider the issue of 'Why me?' This question is an auspicious sign. Tomorrow we shall talk all about it. Let us conclude our meeting for today.'

Hercules left everyone in confusion. They were keen to understand the eternal question of 'Why me?'

Tulsi couldn't sleep that night. She sat up in her bed, took her diary and pen, and started writing.

- After last year's accident, I was transferred to this place. Until then I had not left my ancestral home. Here, I am living an independent life. This has increased my self-confidence.

- Due to the problem in my leg, I am more conscious of doing my work responsibly and well, lest anyone accuse me of using my accident as an excuse to avoid work.

- Here I have found close friends like Rukmini and Urmila with whom I can share my pain and sorrow.

- After coming here, I have had the good fortune of meeting Hercules who is imparting great wisdom and opening up new dimensions of life.

- I have got an opportunity to discover the truth of life through contemplation.

- Truly, the road accident is proving to be instrumental in transforming my life. I need to pay attention to this aspect of my accident. I need to not only forgive that motorcyclist but also be grateful to him.

Thereafter she drifted into sleep.

Hercules too couldn't sleep. His mind was stuck in the past. After coming to know about Tulsi, he understood the secret of god's divine plan and how people become instrumental for each other's growth. What a great arrangement god has made! Can this be anything but grace?

The next evening, Tulsi read out her contemplation to everyone. Hercules smiled. The others too saw a new perspective in her thoughts. Then Tulsi said, 'I am very keen to hear the rest of yesterday's incomplete sermon. Even though I have started thinking positively, I still wonder why this had to happen to me.'

'Today I have brought the book, *The Path to Peace*, with me. This is my guru,' said Hercules. He spread a clean white piece of cloth and kept the book on it. 'Today we shall read about the answers related to your question.' He opened the book, paid respects to it and started reading.

EVERYTHING IS A GAME OF BELIEFS; UNDERSTANDING IS COMPLETE IN ITSELF.

> The deepest and root belief is living life considering yourself to be your body. In reality, you are not the body—you are the life entity called consciousness. The body is just an instrument for the consciousness to experience itself. Just as a mirror is a means to show you your face, your body is a means to show you your real self, i.e. consciousness. But man forgets this and lives his life considering his self to be the body.

Everyone looked at each other in wonder. Hercules continued reading.

> If you consider your self to be your body, then you will want some comfort, some convenience, some freedom and some pleasure for your body. You won't want anything more than this. These are the only desires that will arise if you consider your self to be the body. But now you have to realize what you really are. This is your most important task. Until now you thought that you were the body, but the truth is that you are the experience of being alive, which is beyond the body. You can know this formless experience by making use of this body as an instrument. You consider your body, mind or intellect to be you, but you are none of these. Your real existence is beyond these. When you say, "This is my shirt, this is my pen," it means you are separate from these things, and you agree with that. But when you say, "This is my body," you fall into the illusion that you are the body. Isn't this interesting?

'If I am not the body, mind or intellect, then who am I?' asked Rukmini.

'This has been explained,' Hercules said. 'Please listen.'

> The consciousness that is saying, 'This is my body,' is what you are. It is important to remember this I-am-ness. Let us understand this better with the help of an example. An individual said four sentences about himself after an incident:
>
> 1. I went to the roof.
>
> 2. My hand got injured.
>
> 3. I felt bad.

4. I thought of going to the doctor.

When he said, 'I went to the roof,' he used the word 'I' for his body. Similarly, we also often speak considering ourselves to be the body, such as, 'I had food,' 'I drank water,' 'I went,' 'I came,' 'I laughed,' 'I cried,' etc.

In the second sentence, he said, 'My hand got injured.' Here he is considering himself to be separate from his body. You call something 'mine' only when you regard yourself as separate from it. When you say, 'my hand,' 'my shirt,' 'my mike,' etc. it becomes clear that you are separate from these objects. In other words, there is someone else here who is separate from the body.

In the third sentence, when he said, 'I felt bad,' he is considering himself to be the mind, because the body cannot feel bad. Only the mind can feel bad. Therefore, understand that when you say things like 'I felt bad' or 'I felt good' you consider yourself to be the mind.

In the fourth sentence, when he said, 'I thought of going to the doctor,' he is considering himself to be the intellect.

In this way, in the course of just one event, he considers himself to be the body, the mind, the intellect, as well as that which he truly is.

Pondering over this, Tulsi said, 'I had an accident. My leg was injured. I felt miserable. After the initial treatment, I decided to go to a physiotherapist to help regain my leg movements. All these sentences reflect what you have just told us.'

'Correct!' said Hercules. 'Now tell me, if you say you are happy, then who are you?'

'Then, I am "I",' said Tulsi thinking hard.

'You're right! You are able to understand the teachings of this book. Now let us proceed further,' said Hercules and resumed reading.

> Here, only four sentences have been used as an example. These four sentences have told you about four types of 'I'. If you reflect in depth, many such 'I's will be revealed to you. Sometimes one 'I' will come up and sometimes another, but you always feel that only one 'I' is speaking. In the crowd of these false 'I's, the real 'I' gets lost.

'How can we know this real "I"?' asked the priest.

'That's what we shall find out now,' said Hercules and continued reading.

> It is very easy as well as very difficult to know the real 'I'. It is difficult because this real 'I' is very close to you—so close that you have never looked that closely before. For example, you keep repeating the four kinds of sentences mentioned earlier, but you never think that, through these sentences, you are considering yourself to be separate from your body, mind or intellect. Do the following exercise whenever you remember to, throughout the day. Whenever you use the words 'I', 'me', 'myself', 'mine', etc. ask yourself, 'Who am I referring to?' Doing this exercise will raise your level of consciousness. When you learn, through investigation, about all that you are not, you will learn who you actually are. Understand that you are merely using your body—you are not the body. When you drive your car, you do not identify with it. You do not say that you are the car. You simply say, 'This is my car.' When you use 'my' or 'mine' with something, that thing cannot be you.

'Tulsi, has your question of "Why me?" been answered?' asked Hercules.

'Yes, I'm beginning to understand that the accident happened to my body and not to me. But I have no experience of this new, real "I".'

'Come, let us perform an experiment to understand this.' Hercules closed the book, asked them all to sit in a posture of meditation and started giving instructions. 'Look at your right hand for some time. Now ask yourself, "Am I this hand?" Wait a while for the answer. Let your experience answer, not your intellect. What relationship do you have with your hand? You will realize, "This is my hand, but I am not the hand." Likewise, perform this exercise with all the various parts of your body, such as your leg, your abdomen, etc. Ask this question for every one of them. "Am I this foot? Am I the abdomen?" Continue this experiment for about ten minutes.' After some time, Hercules asked softly, 'What are you experiencing now?'

Tulsi said, 'This experiment is telling me that I am not these body parts. But then, who am I?'

'Okay. Now keeping your eyes closed, ask yourself, "If my hand is amputated, will I remain or not?" Wait for a while to receive the answer.' After a pause, Hercules said, 'The answer will come, "No, I am still complete. I do not feel incomplete even after losing a hand." When someone loses his limbs in an accident, he still feels complete. He doesn't say, "I am half." Because when the body is cut, you do not get cut. When you start experiencing this truth, then your root belief of "I am the body" will break.'

'Oh!' Tulsi's eyes filled with tears. 'Nature has made me experience this already, but it is giving me the understanding today. I understand now that my I-am-ness didn't get fractured when the bones of my leg got fractured. My inner experience remained the same before and after the accident.'

There was stillness all around. Everyone's eyes were closed. Everybody's experience dissolved in Tulsi's experience. Even after dissociating from the body, they were all experiencing themselves. Hercules looked at them and closed his eyes as well. After some time, they became aware of the world once more. They waited for Hercules' next instruction. Hercules said softly, 'Now my purpose of coming here has been fulfilled. Tomorrow, the priest and I will leave for the temple.'

Over the past few days everyone had gotten used to the evening sessions. They were saddened by the news of Hercules' departure. After a while, Rukmini earnestly thanked Hercules and said, 'Whatever we have heard from you until now has brought about a great change in us. Now we want to experience the real "I" and achieve liberation from the root belief.'

'Keep investigating within. This investigation will take you forward,' said Hercules and gave his best wishes to everyone. All of them thanked Hercules one by one.

The next day, Hercules left for the temple along with the priest. While travelling back, Hercules told himself, 'My intuition tells me that Tulsi and Rukmini have received the understanding that I wished to impart to them. So far, eleven people's lives have changed and only one month is left in this year. With the grace of the Goddess, I shall change another person's life in this month and complete my penance.'

One week passed, then another, but he couldn't find the twelfth person anywhere. The priest was not assigning him any task either. Day by day, his restlessness was growing. He was feeling a strange sense of incompleteness. Every moment, his mind was searching for the twelfth one. Worried that his penance would remain incomplete, he couldn't even sleep well.

At last, it was the 11th of December. The next day would mark the completion of a full year of penance, but he still hadn't found his twelfth man. The temple's annual festival was also scheduled for the 12th. Hercules prepared for the festival in a half-hearted, resigned manner. He somehow got through the day, but at night his desperation reached fever pitch. His mind kept asking, 'Who's the twelfth?' Worried about his repentance and about displeasing the mother goddess, he meditated to get rid of his anxiety.

He prayed to the Goddess to reveal the mystery. Then, from the depths of his trance, he heard a divine voice, 'The one who changed eleven lives is the twelfth man! You are the twelfth person!'

The mystery was solved. The dam of emotions finally broke and tears started rushing down his cheeks. He didn't try to stop them. He let whatever was happening happen. He was absorbed in the experience of being. Time stood still. He didn't know how much time elapsed in this state of self-realization. An indescribable bliss pervaded his being. 'I am the twelfth. And I am the first! Without the first, how could the others come? Where did this first one come from? The truth is that I was here all along. Did the fire of penance reveal the first one? It means that this penance has been a medium for attaining unlimited bliss. And this body, the medium for receiving this bliss.'

An eternal spring of understanding and a fountain of wisdom burst forth.

Today was the 12th of December. It was the day of the annual festival at the temple. Every year, this day was celebrated with great pomp and show. According to tradition, the priest used to organize this festival in a big way with help from the villagers. Although earlier it was just a facade for him, things were different this year. The priest had arranged for this year's function with a pure heart and open mind. The temple and its precincts were lavishly decorated. An attractive canopy was erected. There were twinkling lights all around. A great crowd of devotees had gathered like every year. The deity was going to be anointed and adorned after which there would be prayers, worship rituals and offerings. Hymns would be sung throughout the day. Arrangements for distributing the offerings to all the devotees were also made. Hercules had especially invited Jitendra, Mahesh, Angad, Alok, Pooja, Jessica, Mr Srinivasan, Gayatri Devi, Rukmini and Tulsi.

All of them had accepted Hercules' invitation and joined the festivities with full devotion. Hercules and the priest were busy with the programme all day. Therefore, Hercules had not found a chance to converse with his special invitees, who wanted to share the joy that they had achieved after self-exploration.

In the evening, the function ended and the crowd thinned out. That was when the priest and Hercules got some free time. The special guests expressed their desire to speak to Hercules separately. Hercules requested them to spend the night there and arranged for a meeting with them after dinner.

After dinner, all of them gathered in the courtyard of the temple. The temple was bathed in the bright light of the full moon and a spectacular fountain added to the beauty of the surroundings. The silvery moonlight was spreading peace and joy all around. Everyone's face reflected their happiness and contentment. All the twelve people—the ten guests, the priest and Hercules—sat down in a circle. Hercules introduced the guests to the priest and asked them to narrate their experiences one by one, so that the others too could derive inspiration.

Jitendra began, 'Through investigation, I have realized that we should refrain from blaming each other, especially in marital relations, and concentrate upon improving our own selves. This understanding has helped bring back love and warmth in our relationship. We are both over the moon!' Everyone laughed with pleasure.

Mahesh said that his investigation helped him get rid of all his job-related issues once and for all. Maya had also managed to get rid of her habit of getting excited and worried at every little thing.

Angad and Jessica described how their thoughts related to injustice were resolved through inner investigation. Alok said, 'My belief that people are partial is eliminated. Now I interact with people with good feelings and I get ample proof to strengthen my new beliefs.' Jessica said, 'The event related to my landlord's injustice made me realize that I needed to stop committing injustices against myself, only then will others stop their injustices towards me.'

Mr Srinivasan and Gayatri Devi spoke about their health-related investigation. They explained how the experience of the body and that of the self are different from each other.

Rukmini said, 'I used to consider myself highly capable. But after investigation I came to know of many areas where I was totally incompetent.'

Tulsi's account was the epitome of how to forgive after letting go of the trauma caused by an accident.

After listening to all the guests, the priest presented his story. For a moment they were all stunned by his confessions, but later they couldn't help admiring his courage. The courage to face himself in the truest sense made him the object of everyone's admiration. They all gave him a standing ovation. One of them said, 'Being in the presence of a great man like Hercules and receiving guidance from him has transformed our lives. We cannot thank him enough!'

Listening to everyone, glimpses of his past life appeared before Hercules' eyes. He had made a U-turn in his life and had helped bring about a change in so many people's lives. He felt overwhelmed by the infinite divine grace. He was immensely grateful that the Goddess transformed his life and made him instrumental in transforming the lives of eleven others.

But now it was his turn. He requested everyone to remain seated and related his story—his previous life, his broken family, his disputes with his business partner, his bad relationship with everyone. And the dark night when his carelessness caused the road accident.

Tulsi heard the last sentence and couldn't believe her ears. She stared at him in utter shock. When she recovered, she clenched her fists in rage. All her understanding and learning evaporated in that moment. She started spewing venom, 'You cheat! Liar! Hypocrite! Why did you keep your reality hidden until now? You preach the virtue of honesty, then why didn't you reveal your misdeeds when you were at our place? You were scared that no one would listen to you then, no one would consider you great, no one would honour you so much! Just remember, you can't become a saint after committing such a crime. You will definitely reap its bitter fruit!'

All the others were frozen with disbelief. They looked as though struck by lightning. A storm of thoughts broke in their minds. 'Is he really a cheat and a hypocrite? Are we being made a party to some fraud? Can a criminal be a true guide?'

Despite Tulsi's furious outburst, Hercules remained calm. He knew that Tulsi would get over it. The darkness of ignorance cannot survive in the light of contemplation for long. The priest too remained steadfast despite the reaction of the others. His faith in Hercules didn't waver one bit. He had faith in his own experience. He calmed everyone and said, 'At this moment, when you should be using your powers of discrimination, you are entertaining negative thoughts. History is replete with examples of great men who were sinners in their early lives or were living under the influence of their tendencies, aspirations and sensuous pleasures. But upon the awakening of their consciousness, they lived a pure and detached life—like a lotus flower. Valmiki, the creator of the Ramayana, used to be a dacoit. One question from Narada changed his life forever. Lord Buddha led a life of luxury in his earlier years. On encountering sickness, old age and death, he got scared. This fear made him investigate within and he achieved enlightenment. King Asoka waged several wars in order to expand his empire, but one day the horrors of war made him take a vow to work for the welfare of people. He spent his remaining life propagating peace through Buddhism. Similarly, a prostitute spent the rest of her life spreading truth, inspired by Buddha's teachings. Therefore, do not judge people by their pasts. Just pay attention to their present conduct.'

The priest's words cooled the atmosphere a bit. Tulsi's anger had reduced somewhat, but the situation was still too much for her and she walked out. Given the delicacy of the situation, the priest gently adjourned the meeting and everyone agreed to meet again in the morning.

Staying arrangements for the special guests had been made in the temple premises. However, sleep was far from them. What had happened was simply unimaginable. They were staggered by Hercules' disclosure. They used to consider him a superman. He was almost like a god to them, because he was able to guide them all in the best possible manner. But after hearing his truth, his immaculate image took a beating. They all kept tossing and turning through the night.

In the women's chamber, Tulsi was pacing the room in agitation. Her thoughts were unstoppable. 'Oh god, what kind of test is this? What the priest said is true, but why can't I accept it? I'm extremely hurt by Hercules' confession. So am I considering myself to be the mind? If I am not the mind, who am I? Just as I could experience myself even after breaking my leg, I can experience myself even after the shattering of my mind. Then why am I complaining? When I am complaining, what am I considering myself to be? Who is Tulsi? Is she merely a teacher? Or a woman? Or a tenant? Or a friend? Aren't all these mere labels? It is due to these labels that honour and humiliation, love and hate, joy and sorrow exist. Then who am I?

'The meditation Hercules taught us makes us forget the existence of our body. We go beyond name and form. Am I that experience? Our body keeps changing while passing through various stages of life such as childhood, adulthood and old age. External events keep changing and accordingly, our inner feelings, thoughts and desires also change. But our inner self is unchangeable. It's always the same. It is permanent. The real "I" is that which never changes.

'Just a few hours earlier, my mind was filled with fury after learning the truth about Hercules. It spoke ruthlessly in anger, but now the state of my mind is different. Everything changes but the real "I" doesn't change. If I remember this real "I" at all times, only then will I be able to see all the forms of my mind as a witness. Then I will be able to remain detached in all circumstances. If that horrible accident caused by Hercules has led to his transformation into a veritable master, can't it also take me to the real "I"? A particular incident can become a stepping stone for one person, and it can become a deep abyss for another. The difference lies in our approach. Hercules renounced his home, family and everything else as repentance for that accident, but I am still holding on to this anger.

'This accident is compelling me to explore my root belief of "I am the body". The fact is that Hercules has proved to be instrumental in awakening my consciousness, but in my ignorance I am considering him to be my enemy. Oh god! What a great sin I was going to commit!'

The light of contemplation gave rise to a new ray of hope even amidst the dense darkness of ignorance. Tulsi dissolved into an extraordinary experience, far away from the world of her body and her thoughts.

In the morning, all of them gathered together in the temple at eight, except Tulsi. All faces showed signs of lack of sleep. However, in spite of repentance, ignorance and guilt, a smile of contemplation peeked through. The priest asked them, 'What is your state this morning?'

'In the beginning our minds were filled with all kinds of doubts and suspicions, but on getting hold of one end of the truth, things began to untangle and finally clarity dawned,' Mahesh said on behalf of everyone.

'Wonderful,' said the priest. 'Now please tell what lines you investigated along to change your internal state.'

One by one, they recounted their final lines of investigation:

- It is a false belief that the one imparting wisdom should necessarily have a pure and spotless past. If Hercules has not lived a spotless life in the past, it doesn't mean that he cannot be trusted. We must give importance to our own-experience and see the transformation that he has brought in our lives.

- We need to investigate: what sins have we committed in our pasts? How many minds have we hurt?

- We are wearing red glasses.

- This is god's play. We are mere puppets.

- An event which makes us unhappy is but an illusory truth. I will look at the only truth—the divine qualities in Hercules, in this case.

- Turn your thoughts upside down.
- This is what I need at this moment.

At this juncture, a calm and collected Tulsi made an entry. As opposed to yesterday's indignation, she looked serene this morning. She went straight to Hercules and offered a heartfelt apology. Without further ado, she requested Hercules to carry on with the rest of his story. This was a pleasant sight for all.

Hercules smiled and said, 'You may have read about the famous Hercules in Greek and Roman legends. That Hercules had committed some sins in his life. As a result, he had to live as a slave to a king, as instructed by the Oracle of Delphi. This was his penance. The king asked him to carry out twelve exceedingly difficult tasks which were beyond an average man's physical and mental capacity. Hercules completed all those tasks with great élan. These tasks are known as Herculean tasks. Likewise, my past life was full of mistakes. Full of repentance, I prayed to the Goddess and she appeared before me. She instructed me to come to this temple and serve the priest. She asked me to obey him and change the lives of twelve people in twelve months. Today I am very happy that I have been able to obey the Goddess and complete my penance. Thanks to the Goddess, my life has been completely transformed. Now I am confident that I can go back and bring my family together again—and make it a happy family. In addition, I shall be working diligently to create a highly evolved society.'

Everyone wanted to know what he meant by a highly evolved society.

In answer to that, Hercules asked them, 'If you consider me your guide, are you ready to help me bring a great plan into action?' All of them expressed their readiness. Hercules said, 'This is my plan. Each person present here today, on the 12th of December, should work at changing twelve lives by the next 12th of December, by teaching them the technique of inner investigation. Whatever you have learnt, you have to teach that to twelve other people. Then come here with those twelve people on the 12th of December next year to celebrate the great festival of a highly evolved society. And then ask those twelve people to change twelve lives each. Let this cycle go on for twelve years.'

The desire to do something great in life shone in everyone's eyes.

'Which means that next year 144 people will be here,' Hercules said.

The priest also calculated in his mind and said excitedly, 'And the year after that, there will be 144 times twelve… which means, 1,728 people.'

Tulsi calculated the figure for the third year on her mobile phone: '248,832—two lakh, forty eight thousand, eight hundred and thirty-two people!'

Everyone was amazed.

Angad took out his calculator and started figuring out the numbers for the years ahead. Everyone looked at him in anticipation. After a few minutes he said, 'I can't believe it! Do you know the number of transformed people after twelve years?'

He didn't prolong the suspense and announced, 'One crore, six lakh, ninety-nine thousand, three hundred and twenty crores! In other words, around 107,000 billion!'

'Unbelievable! Unimaginable! Unfathomable!' Their eyes were popping out. They stood like statues with feelings of astonishment and disbelief.

After revelling in the revelation for a while, Tulsi said, 'The present population of the world is less than seven billion. In twelve years, this population will be approximately eight billion. But the figure calculated by Angad is far greater. That figure will take care of many such worlds.'

Angad chimed in, 'Seven to eight billion people will be covered in just the first eight years. According to my calculation, sixty-one billion people will be changed by the ninth year.'

'Oh my god! Such a huge figure! Actually, the work entrusted to us is not all that difficult. If we can all divide and shoulder our responsibility of changing the world, the task becomes very easy,' said Pooja.

'If our goal can be achieved in just eight years, what will we do for the next four?' asked Jessica.

'Those four years are the grace period,' Hercules laughed, 'to complete any work that still remains after these eight years.'

'I can't believe that twelve people can bring about such a great revolution,' said Gayatri Devi.

Hercules replied, 'One seed can create a large forest. One change has the power to change the whole world. If you have faith, the caravan of truth will begin—just like the twelve disciples of Jesus had started a caravan. If we all start working with commitment and prepare committed people, then this world will soon become a highly evolved society—a world filled with love, peace, happiness and devotion.'

All of them, including the priest, listened to Hercules with complete devotion. They were convinced that, soon, all the people of the world would become proficient in wielding the mirror of inner investigation and resolving all conflicts. They all got up, drawn by their inner calling and started on the path of introducing others to inner exploration...

In the meantime, Hercules called up his wife Radha and assured her that he was a changed man. He described to her how he had recognized and encountered his ego. And, as soon as he accepted his mistakes, he found that love and joy were waiting to welcome him into a new life.

Hercules bade goodbye to the priest and took off for that known yet new world, which would serve as a mirror for 12 more people…

◻ ◻ ◻

You can mail your opinion or feedback on this book to:
books.feedback@tejgyan.org

About Sirshree

Sirshree's spiritual quest, which began during his childhood, led him on a journey through various schools of philosophy and meditation practices. He studied a wide range of literature on mind science and spirituality. After a long period of deep contemplation on the truth of life, his quest culminated in attaining the ultimate truth.

Sirshree espouses, "All spiritual paths that lead to the truth begin differently but culminate at the same point – Understanding. This understanding is complete in itself. Listening to this understanding is enough to attain the Truth." Over the last two decades, he has dedicated his life to raise mass consciousness.

Sirshree has delivered more than 4000 discourses that throw light on this understanding. He has designed a system for wisdom, which makes it accessible to all. This system has inspired people from all walks of life to progress on their journey of the Truth. Thousands of seekers join in a virtual prayer for World Peace and Global Healing daily at 9:09 am and 9:09 pm.

About Tej Gyan Foundation

Tej Gyan Foundation is a non-profit organization founded on the teachings of Sirshree. The Foundation disseminates Tejgyan – the wisdom that guides one from self-development to Self-realization, leading towards Self-stabilization.

The Foundation's system for imparting wisdom has been assessed by international quality auditors and accredited with the ISO 9001:2015 certification. This wisdom has been presented in a simple, systematic, and practically applicable form that makes it accessible to people from all walks of life, regardless of religion, caste, social strata, country, or belief system.

The Foundation has centers in more than 400 cities and towns across India and other countries. The mission of Tej Gyan Foundation is to create a highly evolved society by leading seekers from negative thoughts to positive thoughts and further, from positive thoughts to Happy thoughts. A 'Happy thought' is the auspicious thought of being free from all thoughts, leading to the state of supreme bliss beyond thoughts.

If you seek such wisdom that leads you beyond mere knowledge, dissolves all problems, frees you from all limiting beliefs, reveals the true nature of divinity, and establishes you in the ultimate truth, then it is time to discover Tejgyan; it is time to rise above the mundane knowledge of words and experience Tejgyan!

The MahaAasmani Magic of Awakening Retreat

Self-development to Self-realization towards Self-stabilization

Do you wish to experience unconditional happiness that is not dependent on any reason? Happiness that is permanent and only increases with time? Do you wish to experience love, peace, self-belief, harmony in relationships, prosperity, and true contentment? Do you wish to progress in all facets of your life, viz. physical, mental, social, financial, and spiritual?

If you seek answers to these questions and are thirsty for the ultimate truth, then you are welcome to participate in the MahaAasmani Magic of Awakening retreat organized by Tej Gyan Foundation. This is the Foundation's flagship retreat based on the teachings of Sirshree.

The purpose of this retreat

The purpose of this retreat is that every human being should:

- Discover the answer to "Who am I" and "Why am I?" through direct experience and be established in ultimate bliss.

- Learn the art of living in the present, free from the burden of the past and the anxiety of the future.

- Acquire practical tools to help quieten the chattering mind and dissolve problems.

- Discover missing links in the practices of Meditation (*Dhyana*), Action (*Karma*), Wisdom (*Gyana*), and Devotion (*Bhakti*).

About Books by Sirshree

Sirshree's published work includes more than 150 book titles, some of which have been translated into more than 10 languages. His literature provides a profound reading on various topics of practical living and unravels the missing links in karma, wisdom, devotion, meditation, and consciousness.

His books have been published by leading publishing houses like Penguin, Hay House, Bloomsbury, Wisdom Tree, Jaico, etc. "The Source" book series, authored by Sirshree, has sold over 10 million copies. Various luminaries and celebrities like His Holiness the Dalai Lama, publishers Mr. Reid Tracy, Ms. Tami Simon and Yoga Master Dr. B. K. S. Iyengar have released Sirshree's books and lauded his work.

The Source
Attain Both, Inner Peace and Worldly success

Awaken the Power of Faith
Discover the 7 Principles of the Highest Power of the Universe

To order books authored by Sirshree, login to:
www.gethappythoughts.org
For further details, call: +91 9011013210

SELECT BOOKS AUTHORED BY SIRSHREE

  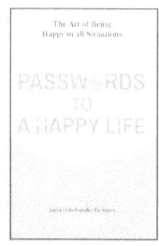 

   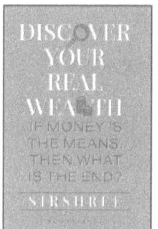

  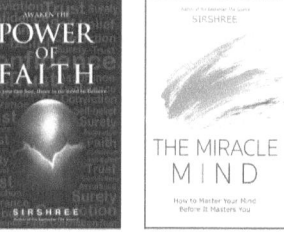 

To order these and other books authored by Sirshree
Visit **www.gethappythoughts.org**

Tej Gyan Foundation – Contact details

Registered Office:
Happy Thoughts Building, Vikrant Complex, Near Tapovan Mandir, Pimpri, Pune 411017, INDIA. Contact: +91 20-27411240, +91 20-27412576

MaNaN Ashram:
Survey No. 43, Sanas Nagar, Nandoshi Gaon, Kirkatwadi Phata, Off Sinhagad Road, Taluka Haveli, Pune district - 411024, INDIA. Contact: +91 992100 8060.

WORLD PEACE PRAYER

Divine Light of Love, Bliss, and Peace is Showering;

The Golden Light of Higher Consciousness is Rising;

All negativity on Earth is Dissolving;

Everyone is in Peace and Blissfully Shining;

O God, Gratitude for Everything!

Members of Tej Gyan Foundation have been offering this impersonal mass prayer for many years. Those who are happy can offer this prayer. Those feeling low or suffering from illness can receive healing with this prayer.

If you are feeling troubled or sick, please sit to receive the healing effect of this prayer. Visualize that the divine white healing light is being showered on earth through the prayers of thousands and is also reaching you, bringing you peace and good health. You can dwell in this feeling for some time and then offer your gratitude to those offering the prayer.

A Humble Appeal

More than a million peace lovers pray for World Peace and Global Healing every morning and evening at 9:09. Also, a prayer (in Hindi) to elevate consciousness is webcast every day on YouTube at 3:30 pm and 9:00 pm IST. Please participate in this noble endeavor.

www.ingramcontent.com/pod-product-compliance
Lightning Source LLC
LaVergne TN
LVHW041708070526
838199LV00045B/1262